THIRD-DEGREE
BROWN BELT
SUDOKU®

FRANK LONGO

MARTIAL ARTS SUDOKU

BROWN

HARD

PUZZLE
WRIGHT
PRESS

An imprint of Sterling
Publishing Co., Inc.
www.puzzlewright.com

CONTENTS

Introduction
3

Puzzles
5

Answers
155

Puzzlewright Press and the distinctive Puzzlewright Press logo are registered trademarks of Sterling Publishing Co., Inc.

2   4   6   8   10   9   7   5   3

Published by Sterling Publishing Co., Inc.
387 Park Avenue South, New York, NY 10016
© 2009 by Sterling Publishing Co., Inc.
Distributed in Canada by Sterling Publishing
c/o Canadian Manda Group, 165 Dufferin Street
Toronto, Ontario, Canada M6K 3H6
Distributed in the United Kingdom by GMC Distribution Services
Castle Place, 166 High Street, Lewes, East Sussex, England BN7 1XU
Distributed in Australia by Capricorn Link (Australia) Pty. Ltd.
P.O. Box 704, Windsor, NSW 2756, Australia

Sterling ISBN 978-1-4027-4648-2

For information about custom editions, special sales, premium and
corporate purchases, please contact Sterling Special Sales
Department at 800-805-5489 or specialsales@sterlingpublishing.com.

INTRODUCTION

To solve sudoku puzzles, all you need to know is this one simple rule:

Fill in the boxes so that the nine rows, the nine columns, and the nine 3×3 sections all contain every digit from 1 to 9.

And that's all there is to it! Using this simple rule, let's see how far we get on this sample puzzle at right. (The letters at the top and left edges of the puzzle are for reference only; you won't see them in the regular puzzles.)

The first number that can be filled in is an obvious one: box EN is the only blank box in the center 3×3 section, and all the digits 1 through 9 are represented except for 5. EN must be 5.

	A	B	C	D	E	F	G	H	I
J									
K					2		1	8	4
L	9		5		7		2		6
M	1		4	3	9	2		7	
N				7		6			
O		7		1	4	8	9		2
P	3		2		6		8		5
Q	8	4	9		3				
R									

The next box is a little trickier to discover. Consider the upper left 3×3 section of the puzzle. Where can a 4 go? It can't go in AK, BK, or CK because row K already has a 4 at IK. It can't go in BJ or BL because column B already has a 4 at BQ. It can't go in CJ because column C already has a 4 at CM. So it must go in AJ.

Another box in that same section that can now be filled is BJ. A 2 can't go in AK, BK, or CK due to the 2 at EK. The 2 at GL rules out a 2 at BL. And the 2 at CP means that a 2 can't go in CJ. So BJ must contain the 2. It is worth noting that this 2 couldn't have been placed without the 4 at AJ in place.

Many of the puzzles rely on this type of steppingstone behavior.

We now have a grid as shown.

Let's examine column A. There are four blank boxes in column A; in which blank box must the 2 be placed? It can't be AK because of the 2 in EK (and the 2 in BJ). It can't be AO because of the 2 in IO. It can't be AR because of the 2 in CP. Thus, it must be AN that has the 2.

	A	B	C	D	E	F	G	H	I
J	4	2							
K					2		1	8	4
L	9		5		7		2		6
M	1		4	3	9	2		7	
N				7	5	6			
O		7		1	4	8	9		2
P	3		2		6		8		5
Q	8	4	9		3				
R									

3

By the 9's in AL, EM, and CQ, box BN must be 9. Do you see how?

We can now determine the value for box IM. Looking at row M and then column I, we find all the digits 1 through 9 are represented but 8. IM must be 8.

This brief example of some of the techniques leaves us with the grid at right.

You should now be able to use what you learned to fill in CN followed by BL, then HL followed by DL and FL.

As you keep going through this puzzle, you'll find it gets easier as you fill in more. And as you keep working through the puzzles in this book, you'll find it gets easier and more fun each time. The final answer is shown below.

This book consists of 300 puzzles of hard level of difficulty.

—Frank Longo

	A	B	C	D	E	F	G	H	I
J	4	2							
K					2		1	8	4
L	9		5		7		2		6
M	1		4	3	9	2		7	8
N	2	9		7	5	6			
O		7		1	4	8	9		2
P	3		2		6		8		5
Q	8	4	9		3				
R									

	A	B	C	D	E	F	G	H	I
J	4	2	1	6	8	3	5	9	7
K	7	3	6	5	2	9	1	8	4
L	9	8	5	4	7	1	2	3	6
M	1	5	4	3	9	2	6	7	8
N	2	9	8	7	5	6	4	1	3
O	6	7	3	1	4	8	9	5	2
P	3	1	2	9	6	7	8	4	5
Q	8	4	9	2	3	5	7	6	1
R	5	6	7	8	1	4	3	2	9

✓ **1**

1	9	8	4	6	5	7	2	3
3	2	4	8	1	7	6	9	5
7	6	5	9	3	2	1	8	4
2	8	7	3	5	1	4	6	9
9	3	1	2	4	6	5	7	8
5	4	6	7	9	8	2	3	1
6	5	9	1	7	3	8	4	2
4	7	2	5	8	9	3	1	6
8	1	3	6	2	4	9	5	7

✓ **2**

7	5	1	4	6	3	8	2	9
2	4	8	1	5	9	6	3	7
6	3	9	8	2	7	4	1	5
9	2	7	6	4	1	3	5	8
5	6	4	9	3	8	2	7	1
8	1	3	2	7	5	9	6	4
1	9	2	7	8	6	5	4	3
3	7	6	5	9	4	1	8	2
4	8	5	3	1	2	7	9	6

8	2	4	5	1	7	3	9	6
9	6	1	8	2	3	4	7	5
5	7	3	9	4	6	1	2	8
7	1	5	6	3	8	2	4	9
3	4	6	2	7	9	8	5	1
2	9	8	4	5	1	6	3	7
6	5	7	3	8	2	9	1	4
4	3	9	1	6	5	7	8	2
1	8	2	7	9	4	5	6	3

4	9	3	7	6	8	5	1	2
5	1	7	9	3	2	8	6	4
8	6	2	4	5	1	3	7	9
1	5	4	6	2	3	9	8	7
7	3	6	5	8	9	2	4	1
2	8	9	1	4	7	6	5	3
6	2	5	3	7	4	1	9	8
9	4	8	2	1	5	7	3	6
3	7	1	8	9	6	4	2	5

√ **5**

4	3	2	6	7	1	9	8	5
5	8	9	2	4	3	6	1	7
1	7	6	8	9	5	3	4	2
8	2	1	5	3	4	7	9	6
9	5	3	7	1	6	4	2	8
6	4	7	9	8	2	1	5	3
2	6	4	1	5	7	8	3	9
7	1	8	3	2	9	5	6	4
3	9	5	4	6	8	2	7	1

6

4	3	8	1	6	7	2	5	9
1	7	9	2	4	5	6	3	8
5	6	2	3	9	8	7	1	4
8	5	1	4	2	3	9	7	6
3	9	4	6	7	1	8	2	5
7	2	6	5	8	9	3	4	1
2	4	5	8	3	6	1	9	7
6	1	7	9	5	2	4	8	3
9	8	3	7	1	4	5	6	2

7

8	2	9	6	1	7	5	3	4
4	5	3	9	2	8	6	1	7
6	7	1	3	4	5	9	8	2
5	9	2	1	3	4	8	7	6
7	3	8	5	6	9	2	4	1
1	6	4	8	7	2	3	5	9
9	8	7	4	5	6	1	2	3
2	1	6	7	8	3	4	9	5
3	4	5	2	9	1	7	6	8

8

2	5	7	9	8	3	4	6	1
6	1	4	5	2	7	3	9	8
9	8	3	1	4	6	5	2	7
5	679	2	4	1678	8	179	8	3
3	791	18	2	178	5	179	4	6
4	67	18	136	1678	9	17	5	2
7	2	9	8	3	4	6	1	5
8	4	6	7	5	1	2	3	9
1	3	5	69	69	2	8	7	4

9

			1	3	2578	6	57	57
		7	25	9	6	8	4	1
1	6	58	578	458	4578	9	2	3
8	235	1	4	6	2357	235	9	257
		6		1		1		
	7				9	4		6
7	1	2	3589	458	3458	35	6	
6	8	3	59	2	45	7	1	459
59	59	4	6	7	1	23	38	28

10

			5				8	
	6		1					3
		8				9		
5				8		2		6
4								7
1		9		5				8
		2				6		
6					7		1	
	5				2			

				2			5	
		8		3	7			9
		5	6			4		3
		2	3					6
4								7
6					1	9		
5		4			2	3		
8			4	6		7		
	6			8				

	3	5			4			1
		4			1	8	3	
8								
4	2			7	5	6		
6								8
		9	8	6			5	4
								5
	8	1	9			4		
5			4			7	8	

				2		7		3
					5		8	2
			1			9		4
			2		8	4		7
6		4	5		3			
1		5			9			
2	4		3					
3		7		1				

7				6				3
	3		5		4		8	
	6	5	3					
4		6						
3	7						1	8
						3		4
					6	8	2	
	5		1		3		7	
8				5				1

						6	1	
1			9					8
5			3		1		9	
					3		6	2
		6		9		5		
7	9		6					
	2		7		8			9
9					5			6
	4	3						

3	8	1						
		4			5	8		6
					4		7	
2			7	6				1
			1		2			
4				5	8			7
	9		4					
1		2	8			7		
						9	1	8

17

5				7			1	8
	3		8					4
2	8				9	3		
	9		6					
				4				
					8		5	
		9	5				8	1
3					7		9	
8	6			9				2

18

9			3				5	6
						3		8
	8			2	6			
		9	2	6				
7		5				9		2
				4	9	6		
			1	9			8	
1		8						
3	4				8			1

	4	7	2	5				
			7					4
	8				6	2		
			8					6
1								2
7					1			
		6	1				4	
3					9			
				2	4	1	5	

	7	4	6			9	5	
	5							
1		9		5		6		
3					7	1		
7				2				4
		5	4					6
		3		1		4		5
							1	
	8	1			6	7	9	

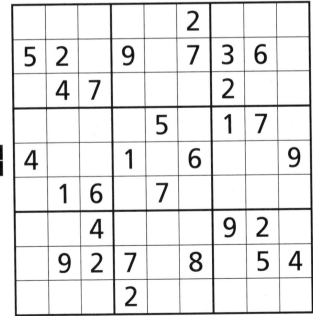

Puzzle 2-1

9				7	5	1		4
7	3							
					9	8		
6	4		5					8
				3				
3					2		4	5
		7	6					
							6	1
1		5	9	4				3

Puzzle 2-2

					2			
					2			
5	2		9		7	3	6	
	4	7				2		
				5		1	7	
4			1		6			9
	1	6		7				
		4				9	2	
	9	2	7		8		5	4
			2					

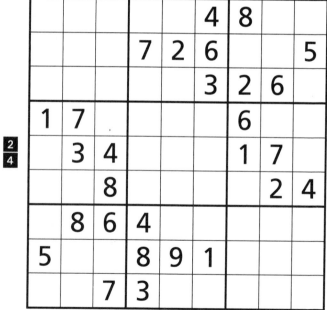

5				1	6		2	7
	8	7			3			5
		6						
	4		3					
7								8
					4		5	
						9		
1			8			2	7	
8	2		1	9				6

1		2			6			
			1	4	7		9	5
					5		1	7
	4	1				8	2	
2	6		8					
7	8		9	3	2			
			6			3		9

		2		9				
5		3					4	
	1		3		4			
7				1	3			
	2	6				7	3	
			2	4				9
			4		6		9	
	9					2		6
				7		1		

			6	4				
7	3				5			
5			8			2		
		2			9			6
	1						9	
8			2			5		
		3			8			4
			7				3	9
				3	6			

	7						8	
		3	5	1				
		1	4	9				
		4				9		1
6								2
9		5				3		
				8	5	7		
				3	6	5		
	3						6	

3								
	7				2		4	9
		2		9			6	8
					4			
1		9	6		7	8		4
			5					
9	3			5		7		
6	2		3				5	
								2

3-1

				3				7
	9			1			3	
7			8	2		9	4	5
					1	8		
9								4
		5	3					
5	1	8		4	3			6
	7			9			8	
2				7				

3-2

5								
3			4	5	1		9	
			3		8			
	3		7	2			1	6
	2	8				5	7	
1	5			8	9		3	
			5		4			
	4		8	7	2			3
								7

Puzzle 33

4				6				
	1	6						7
			3		1	6	2	
	2	5	8				4	
				4				
	8				6	3	5	
	6	3	2		4			
5						7	6	
			5					1

Puzzle 34

	5					6		
	3	8			5		7	
			6	8				5
				1		4		7
	6						1	
8		7		9				
5				4	9			
	9		1			3	6	
		3					5	

4	6							7
1				7	3		6	
		8	6			5	4	
	7	2						
8								3
				6	9			
	5	1			4	8		
	7		8	2				6
2							9	5

			8	9		5		
7	1					2		
					2		8	
3		4	9			7	1	
8								4
	2	1			7	3		5
	8		5					
		7					5	1
		2		7	9			

9								
5		2	9	8		6		
		3					1	
		1	3		8	5		
6				4				2
		8	5		9	7		
	4					1		
		6		1	2	9		4
								7

	9				4	8		
		3				9	4	
		2		9			1	7
	5							3
			8		6			
2							7	
4	6			5		2		
	3	9				6		
		8	6				3	

Puzzle 4/1:

9	5				6		4	
				2		6		
6		8	4	3				
		3	7			8	9	
	7	9			2	5		
			8	3	2			6
		6	5					
	9		6				8	1

Puzzle 4/2:

					7	4		6
		6				1		8
7	8				1		2	
			6			2		9
	6			1			3	
5		2			8			
	9		1				5	2
1		5				8		
6		8	2					

4 3

	7		2					9
		9		1				
	1			7	3	5		
8	2	1						
3								2
						4	6	3
		8	7	3			2	
				6		3		
7					2		5	

4 4

				2	1			
			5			9		1
2					4	3	6	
	7					2		
	3	8	2		6	1	9	
		2					8	
	1	7	6					2
5		6			2			
			8	9				

2		7				5		
9		5			6		1	8
					9			
			6					4
		8	3	1	2	6		
5				8				
			4					
3	5		1			7		6
		2				3		9

	6				3			5
		8				7	4	
1			6	4		3		
								2
	3	4		6		8	1	
5								
		3		9	8			7
	1	5				9		
9			5				6	

4 / 7

9		3		4				
		7					8	
5			7					
8	9				1	4	6	
7								9
	5	4	6				1	2
					4			1
	1					2		
				1		7		5

4 / 8

6	9							
	7	3		8				
	5		7		3			
		6	5				3	9
			6		2			
8	3				9	6		
			2		1		7	
				9		4	6	
							5	8

	7					4		1
		8				6	9	
	3		1					5
		5	4		7			
			5	1	9			
			6		3	8		
3					1		6	
	2	7				9		
5		1					4	

2		3		6				4
			8			7		
	5				9	8	1	
							3	1
		2				9		
1	7							
	4	6	7				8	
		7			1			
5				4		3		7

5/1

7		4	1		6			
3			5	4		7		6
				7		4		
						1		3
2	3						5	9
6		1						
		8		9				
4		3		6	1			7
			7		3	9		4

5/2

	3		2		4			5
						3		
				3	5	8	1	
		5	3					2
	2						6	
8					6	1		
	1	9	4	6				
		3						
4			8		1		7	

5/3

	6	4				1		
			2					4
			5	9		3		7
			9	2		6	1	
				7				
	2	6		4	8			
3		9		5	6			
4					9			
		1				4	9	

5/4

		4			7		8	
1	8							
	7	6	4					
5				6			7	
7			2	4	1			3
	3			7				6
					3	7	6	
							9	2
	1		7			8		

5/5

				8			4	3
4				7				
	5					2	6	
	4		2			5	3	
1								5
		3	8		1		9	
		5	6				8	
				3				9
2	7			5				

5/6

		3	6		9		4	
							1	
2	8		4		5			9
3		9	8				6	
	1				4	9		3
6			9		7		5	1
	9							
	2		3		8	7		

Puzzle 57:

					9			
9		5		4	7			1
	4			5		3	9	
4		2					1	
	5			2			8	
	7					4		5
	6	7		1			3	
2			7	8		6		4
			2					

Puzzle 58:

	4		5	9			7	
		2			8		9	
8			6	1				
	5					3		
3	8						6	4
		6					5	
				5	6			7
	1		4			9		
	2			8	1		4	

					3		6	
7	6							
	8		6		9	5	4	
		2		7		6		
4	7						5	3
		5		2		7		
	2	8	4		7		9	
							7	5
	3		8					

		1		6		9		
			8					
	6		2					4
3			6	1		7		8
1		6				3		9
4		8		7	3			6
9					8		2	
					7			
		7		2		8		

6/1

	9				1		4	7
			9					
	2			4	6			
7		5		6	4			
3			5		2			1
			3	8		5		6
			4	9			2	
				3				
8	3		7				1	

6/2

							6	
7	9		1	2		3		
8		3			4			
	4				7			6
		9				8		
1			5				3	
			2			9		1
		1		9	8		4	5
	5							

6 / 3

		3			9	5		
	4	9						
	6		8	4				
7		6		1	2			
2								3
			7	5		6		2
				6	5		3	
						7	4	
		5	4			1		

6 / 4

	7		6		9	5		8
		4	3			7		
	8					9		
5					8			6
	1						8	
4			2					9
		7					9	
		9			2	6		
1		3	9		6		4	

			7				3	8
				1				
		7		8	3	9	1	
		1	2			7		
	4			3			8	
	8				5	1		
	2	3	8	6		4		
				4				
6	8				2			

3				4		8		
	5		2					
	4				1			2
				9		1	8	3
	2						9	
5	9	1		3				
2			7				6	
					5		7	
		9		1				5

		2	6					
6			1					
		8		4		1		7
		9			7		5	
4	8						3	2
	3		4			9		
5		7		8		2		
					5			8
				9		4		

	4		1			7		
		3	6			2		
7					5			
	5				6	3		
	6	1				9	8	
		4	2				7	
			5					2
		2			9	4		
		9			7		5	

			2					8
5			9		1	2		
					3	9	7	
	8		1	9				6
			6		8			
1				4	5		3	
	4	7	3					
		9	5		4			2
2					9			

			7		6			
2								7
	6			5				4
7	3			2			4	
6		9	3		5	1		2
	4			9			5	3
4				6			3	
9								1
			4		3			

Puzzle 7/1:

							2	
	3	2	9				5	4
6			8					9
			6	5			7	3
		5		1		9		
3	2		4	9				
5					6			8
2	9				4	7	3	
	6							

Puzzle 7/2:

			1	6		8	4	
	1		2				6	
					7			2
1				5		2		
	9						7	
		4		3				1
8			3					
	3				5		8	
	2	6		1	8			

			1				9	7
					6			8
6	3			9				2
		1	5	2			3	
	5			7	9	8		
2				8			4	9
1			9					
3	9				1			

9		2				8		
		4	6			7		
3					9	1	2	
5				9	7		6	
	4		5	2				7
	5	1	2					8
		3			5	6		
		7				4		2

7/5

				9				4
		7	6	4			8	
1		2		7				
7			9	1			4	
		5				7		
	3			5	7			8
				2		8		3
	9			8	5	4		
6				3				

7/6

	9				1	8	3	
	3						4	9
		8		3		5		
7			1		4			
		6		5		7		
			6		2			8
		3		1		2		
8	2						7	
	6	9	7				5	

8				4			2	
		2			7			
	7		2			4		8
	4			1		7		
	5	8				9	4	
		1		8			3	
2		3			9		7	
			3			1		
	9			7				3

		7	1		6			4
		6	4				3	5
2								
		1	3					
5		2				4		6
					2	1		
								2
7	4				5	8		
6			8		9	5		

4			2		3			
	2							6
3	7	9	8					
2	8		6					3
		6				1		
7					8		9	2
					2	4	3	1
8							6	
			1		4			7

7	8		9				4	6
								3
1			7			2		
	2		4	6		3		
5				1				2
		6		9	7		1	
		8			9			4
9								
3	4				6		2	8

Puzzle 8/1

		1						
		9	1				3	2
6		7		4		8		9
					6	7		
			7	5	2			
		6	8					
1		3		8		9		5
8	4				9	2		
						3		

Puzzle 8/2

9						1	6	2
			8		1	5		
	2						7	
	4		6				1	
		8		1		9		
	5				9		2	
	7						9	
		2	7		5			
4	1	3						7

Puzzle 8/3

	7	6		8	9		1	
3			1		6		2	
			2		3	7		
	6	9						
						4	3	
		5	6		8			
	2		9		4			6
	9		5	3		2	4	

Puzzle 8/4

	9				7			
	5		3					1
	8	7	1					4
		5						2
	1		7		3		9	
2						3		
7					5	6	2	
5					9		1	
			6				7	

8/5

1				5			6	3
2					6			
4					1		8	
	1				7			8
7				6				5
8			9				1	
	9		3					6
			6					7
6	7			8				1

8/6

	9				2	5		
5			7	4				9
		1	9					
		4		1				6
	7	5				4	1	
2				6		3		
					5	1		
1				7	4			5
		6	1				3	

1		3		9		5		
9						4	7	
	2			8				
3					2	8		
	4	2		3		6	1	
		1	8					7
				6			5	
	3	4						8
		8		2		1		9

	7			9				
			4				8	
1		4					9	7
	1				5	4	2	
9								3
	6	2	3				7	
4	8					9		2
	3				2			
			7				4	

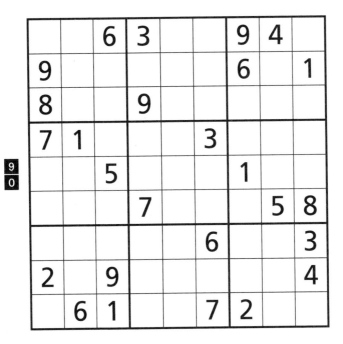

Puzzle 9/1:

							4	
					9		5	1
6	5				1	7		8
5	3		6			9		
	2						8	
		8			7		3	5
8		4	5				9	3
3	9		4					
	1							

Puzzle 9/2:

2	9		3			6	7	
					9			
				6				1
		5	2				9	7
		7				4		
9	8					3	1	
5				7				
			8					
	6	2			5		1	4

9 / 3

	8			9	6			
							9	
6		3	7					4
		7	4		3		5	
	5	2				4	3	
	4		5		2	7		
8					9	5		2
	7							
			2	3			7	

9 / 4

		4		8		6		
		5				2		3
		6	7				4	
1	5				8			
			1	3	5			
			4				2	1
	4				1	8		
7		2				3		
		1		4		7		

						6		2
	8			1				9
	5				3	1	7	8
				7	8			
		8	6		2	7		
			9	5				
1	6	4	8				9	
8				2			6	
7		2						

	2							9
9	6							3
		3	8		6			
		5			1			
6			7	8	4			1
			3			7		
			5		8	2		
3							1	4
8							9	

		8	6			7	3	
				8		9		
	4						2	
3				2		8		
5	8			7			9	1
		9		1				3
	1						7	
		3		9				
	9	4			7	5		

			7					4
	4			9	2			7
		3					1	
		8	5				3	
	3		2	6	1		4	
	9				8	6		
	5					4		
1			4	8			7	
7					3			

2				7		6		
9			4				7	
	6	7					2	1
	7			4	8			2
	8						5	
6			2	9			8	
1	9					8	4	
	2				4			6
		4		8				3

8	4	2						
5			6			7	1	8
			4					
7						8	5	
	5						2	
		6	5					7
					6			
	7	3	2		5			8
						3	1	5

8				2	1			3
		7	3				2	
		4				1		8
9			2					
		3	6	1	9	2		
					8			9
4		9				3		
	7				2	5		
1			9	5				4

			9	1			7	
					8			1
3			7					2
	5			8		9		
	9			7			2	
		4		2			8	
7					2			8
8			3					
	3			6	1			

103

			8		6			1
				4			3	9
	3	6			1		5	
	2				7			8
		3				1		
5			3				2	
	4		1			5	8	
1	5			6				
3			2		5			

104

7	2		6				3	
						4		
		4	2		9			
6	9		1					2
				3		2		
3					6		1	7
			5		4		8	
		6						
	5					7		4	6

Puzzle 105:

		6			4			7
	1		3					
7	4						9	
	5	3		7			4	6
				5				
9	8			6		5	2	
	2						1	4
					2		3	
4			9			2		

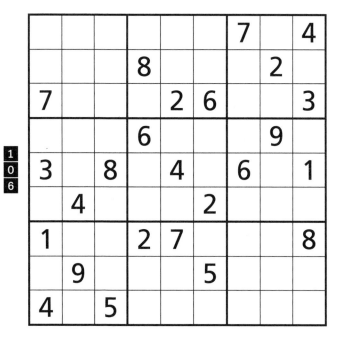

Puzzle 106:

						7		4
			8				2	
7				2	6			3
			6				9	
3		8		4		6		1
	4				2			
1			2	7				8
	9				5			
4		5						

107

			6					7
	9		5	8		4		
					9		3	8
	4	7						2
		9				6		
6						8	7	
9	8		3					
		2		6	1		5	
1					7			

108

	6	7				9		
			6		3		2	
	1			4				
9	7	4						
			7	5	1			
						6	3	7
				7			9	
	8		4		2			
		2				3	1	

3				5					7
7				9			3		
							4		9	2
				5			1		
		3					9		
		4					8		
1	5			3					
				2			9		5
8					1				6

				7	3			2	
		1							5
5							7	9	
	8				1		6	4	
3									2
	4	7		2				3	
	5	8							9
2							8		
	3			9	2				

		6					8	
	2			7		5	3	
		5	4	1	3			
			7			8		
	7			2			5	
		2			9			
			2	6	7	4		
	1	3		5			6	
	6					2		

	5							9
		8		9	3		1	
		7	4					5
		5	2	3	7			
	7						4	
			8	6	4	9		
4				7	5			
	8		3	2		7		
2							3	

	3			6	2	1		
					5			
7			4			9	6	
	2	5						6
9	6						7	2
4						3	8	
	4	7			8			1
			1					
		6	5	2			9	

		8			5	3		
			1					
	1		9	4			5	6
		6	3			9		1
				7				
9		3			1	5		
5	2			1	6		4	
					3			
		1	4			8		

			4		2			
1	3		6			7		
						4		9
8					7	9		5
		1				2		
9		3	5					8
6		7						
		2			9		7	4
			7		8			

8		6				5		
	5	1			3		6	
	2		5					
		5	2	7				4
			3		9			
2				1	6	9		
					1		8	
	8		7			4	5	
		7				2		6

Puzzle 117

	4			3	9			5
			6		1	3		
3							1	
					8	9	7	
1				5				4
	6	4	9					
	1							7
		7	8		2			
2			1	6			5	

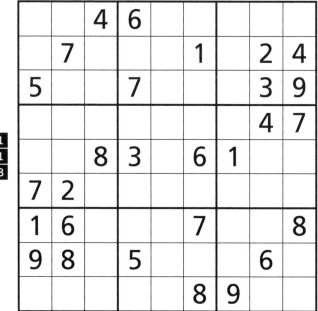

Puzzle 118

		4	6					
	7				1		2	4
5			7				3	9
							4	7
		8	3		6	1		
7	2							
1	6				7			8
9	8		5				6	
					8	9		

	2			6	4		1	
			5			4		
4	9				7	5		
5		7			3			
1								8
			8			2		5
		9	7				5	1
		6			9			
	5		4	3			9	

2			4		3	8		
			6				7	
					2		4	
		2					1	5
9		4		1		7		8
5	6					9		
	2		3					
	4				8			
		7	5		4			1

Puzzle 121

	2			1		5		
9	1		6					
		5	2	4	9			
	9							8
8		2				7		4
6							1	
			5	6	1	9		
					7		2	1
		9		8			7	

Puzzle 122

			9	2	8	5		
				3			6	7
					1		4	
	3	5						1
7								6
1						4	8	
	4		2					
9	7			5				
		3	1	8	4			

Puzzle 1:

	6				8			9
				3			8	
	7		6				5	
7	1	4		5				
5			9		6			1
			2			5	3	7
	5				4		6	
	2			6				
4			2				7	

Puzzle 2:

		6			3		5	
						8		3
		1	2		7			
	8		7	5			6	
		5				2		
	3			1	8		4	
			8		4	9		
5		9						
	7		9			4		

125

	3		5		2			
	7		9	1	8		3	
				3				9
6								8
		1	8		7	5		
2								1
8				7				
	2		6	8	3		9	
			2		4		5	

126

3				4		1		
			8		2			
7					1		4	
5		3						4
		6		7		5		
8						7		1
	1		4					8
			2		7			
		5		6				2

	6	9		2		4		
2					8		6	
			9				2	
4	7			5				
9			8	6	4			5
				9			8	4
	2				9			
	4		2					6
		6		4		1	7	

1	4						7	3
				4		6		
6		9	3			5		
8					1			
			9	3	4			
			2					4
		2			8	3		9
		3		5				
4	6						5	7

1 2 9

						4		
5				4	3		9	
8			7		6			
6	5				7	8		
	8			2			7	
		7	4				1	9
			5		9			4
	4		3	1				6
		6						

1 3 0

	5			7	3	8		
							6	5
	3		5	4			9	
4				9			8	
	7			6				2
	6			2	9		4	
1	4							
		8	4	5			2	

131

1				9				
8		3						
	4	5	1				8	
	3	1			5			6
	7						9	
5			6			1	3	
	5				3	2	4	
						5		9
				4				7

132

					3	5		6
6	4			9			7	
						9		
9	7	8		1				4
3				7		2	6	1
		6						
	2			3			1	9
1		3	7					

133

						5		4
				5			9	
4			2				1	7
8		9	6			2		
3				8				6
		6			2	4		3
5	8				7			2
	1			6				
6		4						

134

				8			2	
	9	2						
7			6			9		
2				3			1	
8		9		4		3		2
	7			5				4
		3			1			8
						5	4	
	4			9				

			1					8
			7				6	9
		4		8		5		7
	3			9				1
		9	3		5	6		
6				4			3	
9		3		6		1		
5	8				9			
1					3			

			4		2			
	7				5	3		1
		5			9			
		9	8				7	3
	1						5	
2	3				1	6		
			1			9		
4		1	2				8	
			9		4			

Puzzle 137:

	5		4	1	6			2
7			9					
	2			7			1	
		1					6	
	9	7		4		3	8	
	3					4		
	6			3			5	
					5			8
5			1	8	4		9	

Puzzle 138:

				3	4			2
	9		7			8	6	
		5	4	1		3	7	
		8		5		1		
	2	1		7	3	9		
	4	9			5		1	
1			3	4				

7		4					5	
8			3			7	4	
1			9					
			5	3			2	4
				1				
3	7			4	9			
					8			5
	8	7			5			6
	6					4		2

							6	
6		7		2				
	5	3		1	9	7		
		6	8				3	
4								2
	7				5	6		
		5	9	6		2	8	
			3			4		9
	8							

	7		6			9		3
				1				7
	4	9	5					
			7	3		8		6
		3				1		
4		7		8	1			
					6	5	3	
8				5				
3		6			8		2	

7		5			4			
	6				1			8
	1		5	8	7			
			7			3		
		6		3		5		
		1			6			
			2	9	3		4	
3			1				2	
			6			9		3

		2	5					
	9			3	1	6		
7							5	
2	3	1		6				7
8								6
6				9		3	2	1
	8							5
		6	7	8			3	
					6	8		

	2	5					4	8
					4	5		
	4		9					6
			6		8	9		
1			4		9			5
		2	5		7			
3					2		8	
		9	8					
2	6					7	3	

				7				
6	2	4	9					
5					6	9		
4			7			6		
	9	2		1		5	7	
		7			2			4
		1	4					6
					7	2	4	8
			5					

	3	5		6	4			
		8	9	7				
9		1					7	
	8		1	5				
4	5						8	1
			4	3		6		
	7					1		5
			2	7		8		
			5	1		6	2	

	4		1		9	7	2	
9			7		2	4	1	
4						5	6	
	1	5				3	4	
	2	6						8
	5	9	3		4			1
	8	1	2		5		3	

					7			
	3	1	2			4		
			4	9		2		5
	9			3	4	7	5	
				8				
	4	5	7	6			3	
1		2		7	5			
		3			8	5	9	
			3					

149

9		3			1			4
		4	7	6				
	8	7					5	
7	6				3			
				5				
			4				2	6
	4					7	6	
				1	7	2		
3			2			8		5

150

			2			7		
	9			1			2	3
5				7		4		
			4	6			8	2
	4						7	
1	2			8	3			
		6		3				4
8	3			4			5	
		9			8			

				4		6	3	9
					9			
8			7					4
				3		1		2
		5				7		
9		3		7				
1					2			7
			8					
2	7	8		5				

9			8				4	1
		3	2	6				
2								
5		9	3					
		1				6		
					7	3		8
								5
				2	5	7		
7	3				9			6

153

1	4							
	6				2			5
		5	6	4			7	
4	9	1		6				
	5						9	
				9		1	5	2
	1			3	6	9		
8			5				6	
							1	4

154

			2	6		5	4	
				5		6	7	
	5				7			8
	3			2	6			
	6		3		1		9	
			9	8			2	
5			4				6	
	4	7		3				
	2	6		1	8			

Puzzle 155

4							7	3
5			4		3	2		
	7		1					
	8						6	4
				1				
7	9						5	
					9		8	
		5	6		4			7
6	4							5

Puzzle 156

				8		5	3	4
9			5					8
		4				6		
					3			6
		5		2		1		
7			4					
		9				2		
8					9			5
1	3	2		6				

82

8	1							
						7	5	
5	2		7	3				
4					3	2		
	5		2	7	1		8	
		1	4					3
				9	5		6	8
	6	8						
							3	2

	8	1			2	3		
				8		4		
			3				2	
	1				4			5
	3	5	2		1	8	6	
6			7				4	
	6				3			
		2		5				
		3	9			2	8	

Puzzle 159:

		1		4	6	8		9
	2					3		
				3	8		5	4
			6					
		2		1		5		
				9				
2	8		9	6				
		5					1	
1		3	7	5		4		

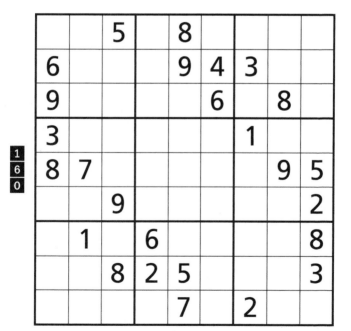

Puzzle 160:

		5		8				
6				9	4	3		
9					6		8	
3						1		
8	7						9	5
		9						2
	1		6					8
		8	2	5				3
				7		2		

	7		1				8	
4						9		
			2					1
	4	9						
1			6		8			7
						2	3	
7				1				
		3						2
	6				4	9		

			2				1	5
				6	1			
	1						7	9
	3	8	7		2		9	
		7				8		
	9		5		3	7	4	
1	5						6	
			1	7				
8	7				4			

		5			9		4	
						3	7	
	1				7			9
	2				8			4
	9	4		2		1	8	
8			6				3	
7			5				9	
	8	9						
	4		9			6		

3					8			
		4		3			5	7
	9	7	4					
4	5	2						
9				2				4
						1	2	3
					7	6	4	
6	4			8		3		
			3					8

	5		3	1				
1	3		2					9
9			7		8			
		9				1		
6	7						3	2
		3				8		
			4		2			5
7					1		2	6
				3	7		9	

			5		2			1
2	6							
7							5	
4			2		5	7	8	
			4		3			
	2	3	7		1			5
	3							7
							2	6
1			3		9			

		7		1	5			
9								8
			2	3		9		4
	6							
5			8		7			6
							3	
1		9		2	4			
4								3
			5	8		1		

		1						5
			1	7	8	3		9
3		7				8		6
	2		8		1			
				9				
			5		2		9	
8		9				6		1
7		2	6	8	3			
4						7		

								4
4				3		7		2
	2			7		6		
			6					9
		1				5		
5					8			
		6		1			9	
1		9		5				8
7								

	9	5	2					
1				5	8			
	7	2		6				
				9		8	3	6
		8				4		
3	5	6		1				
				2		3	8	
			1	8				7
				7	2	4		

	2		3	7				4
			2	1		3	7	
	1					6		
	5	7		4				
		6				7		
				6		8	5	
		9					2	
	8	2	4	9				
5				8	6		3	

		4	7		5	1		
	3		2					
			8			2	7	
							8	5
		6		5		4		
1	5							
	4	3			7			
					4		3	
		5	6		2	8		

Puzzle 173

9			3	4				7
6							1	3
				9				2
	8		1			7	9	
			5		9			
	6	9			3		8	
2				3				
7	5							9
4				5	7			1

Puzzle 174

			2	4			1	7
3						4		2
			3			6		
							9	6
5		9		3		8		1
7	2							
		4			9			
6		1						5
8	3			2	1			

Puzzle 175

							9	
		9	5				2	1
		6	2	9				3
	5		1	4				7
		4				5		
7				6	5		1	
6				8	3	2		
8	4				1	9		
	7							

Puzzle 176

	4	6	1	3		7	9	
	2		4			8		
				6		1		
								4
9			7		5			1
2								
		7		2				
		5			6		2	
	3	2		7	4	6	5	

Puzzle 177:

		5	6			9		
			2			4		6
	7		4		8			
		1						
4		8				5		3
						7		
			7		1		3	
8		7			5			
	5			4		6		

Puzzle 178:

3	2				6			5
				8	5		7	
5		1		7				
	7					9		8
		2				4		
8		3					6	
				6		1		2
	6		8	1				
7			2				9	6

179

	7							5
	6						4	
			4	9	2		8	7
				6	4			8
			3	7	9			
4			5	1				
7	4		1	2	5			
	5						1	
2							9	

180

		5	2	6				4
							1	
	8	6	4				7	9
		9	1		2		6	
				4				
	1		7		6	5		
9	3				4	7	2	
	7							
4				8	7	1		

	9	7		5			1	
					6			
		2				7		
8		6		7	1		4	
		9	5		4	8		
	4		9	8		6		7
		5				1		
			8					
	2			1		4	6	

2		4	6				7	
		6	2				1	
								2
5			1			4		
9			4	3	6			1
		1			7			8
4								
	3				4	1		
	5				9	2		6

183

						3	5	7
	1			7	8	9		
	4							
	8		1		6			5
4								1
7			5		4		8	
							1	
		4	9	5			3	
8	5	6						

184

1			7	3	2		5	
	4				8		3	
		7						8
			8	4	9			
		2		5		3		
		3	2	7				
3						1		
	2		4				9	
	9		6	2	7			3

185

	5				9			
			8			9		7
6			1	5			8	
			4				2	
		6	2	7	3	1		
	2				1			
	7			1	4			6
4		3			5			
			3				1	

186

				4	9		7	
7								9
8	5		6		7			
9		8						
6	3						4	1
						3		7
			7		4		1	2
2								4
	1		8	5				

				2		7	1	
		8				9	4	
			3	4				
	1				3		6	
2		7		5		1		9
	5		2				7	
			3	1				
	8	3				2		
	7	5		6				

2								
	5			8	4	2		7
9			1	2				
	6		3			9	2	
		4		6		8		
	1	2			8		6	
				3	9			4
1		3	4	7			9	
								2

5							8	4
	4			3				
			8			6		5
	5			2			1	9
8				9				3
7	1			8			4	
6		3			4			
				7			3	
4	8							7

6		8				9	7	
					4			
7				2			1	
3					2			
5		9		6		2		3
			7					1
	4			5				9
			9					
	5	1				3		7

7			8	4				
				3				1
	2				5	8		7
2		8				9		
1								2
		3				6		4
5		1	9				7	
6				7				
			6	2				9

5	2			1				9
	3		5					8
	7				2			
	5				8	4		
	6			4			5	
		4	7				8	
			2				9	
3					7		4	
9				8			2	3

Puzzle 193

1		2	3	4			7	
5		9			2		3	
	4				9		6	
6				3				9
	9		7				1	
	6		9			1		8
	5			8	1	2		3

Puzzle 194

	6		4					1
1		2						
7				9			5	4
				9				
9		4	1		2	8		6
			6					
2	7			3				5
						7		3
3					6		8	

4					7	3	1	
			8					7
	8		1					
				9		2		3
		9	7		5	6		
8		4		2				
					1		5	
2					4			
	5	7	6					9

				4		8		
	7		6			4	5	
	8						2	
	2	7		6	9			
	6						1	
			3	8		6	9	
	5						4	
	9	2			4		8	
		1		7				

8	2		9					
	5				7		3	
3				2				
		7			2			
2		4				8		6
			1			5		
				6				9
	3		2				4	
					3		8	5

Puzzle 198

1					9		2	4
		4	6		3			
6								
2			9		4		8	
9	8						4	2
	6		2		1			3
								8
			4		7	3		
3	9		5					7

Puzzle 199

				5		3		
5			3		4			
				2		8		1
	4		6			1		
1	7	9				6	2	4
		6			7		8	
9		4		7				
			1		3			2
		2		6				

Puzzle 200

		2			4		8	
1	5	7				9		
	8		1	6	5			
2	3							
		8		1		7		
							3	1
			6	4	3		1	
		3				6	4	9
	1		8			3		

	7	9		1				
2	6				7			
3			2					6
1				6		9	8	
8			3		1			7
	4	6		9				1
9					2			4
			1				2	9
				7		8	1	

	9	5						
1				2	8			
	6		7				1	
7	2		5					
		3		6		5		
					1		4	9
	3				9		5	
			8	3				1
						6	2	

203

3	5				9		1	
		7					4	
			1			9		
7			4	8				
		5		9		8		
				7	5			2
		4			8			
	3					6		
	7		6				2	8

204

		7	8	9		6		
					1			
5	3						8	
		3		8	2			
		2	4		7	3		
			5	1		9		
	7						3	4
			7					
		6		4	9	1		

2						6	5	4
			5					
	7	5				9		
		6	8	1		4		
	9			7			1	
		1		4	5	7		
		7				2	4	
					8			
8	3	2						1

	6		1		2		8	7
8				6				
3				4		1		
						9	2	
			2		7			
	9	4						
		3		7				4
				5				8
7	1		6		4		9	

						2		
			2			5		9
				7	5			1
7		2		9	6		5	
		9				3		
	4		8	5		1		2
9			5	2				
5		6			3			
		7						

			6			9		
2	8		5				7	
		6					4	3
	9	4			5		2	
				8				
	3		7			4	5	
8	4					7		
	6				8		9	5
		9			3			

							3	
7	5		2				6	
3					1	2		7
				5				8
1	7			4			9	6
9			6					
8		7	3					2
	3				2		7	1
	6							

			2		1		7	
			8				4	
3				5			2	
		4	1		5	9		
		8	6		7	1		
	8			1				7
	9				3			
	5		4		2			

			2	5				
5	9	7			8			
		1					3	
		9		6				1
	5						9	
4				3		8		
	1					4		
			1			9	2	6
				8	5			

			5	7				
2		8						3
					1		6	
3		7		6				9
	1						7	
9				2		3		4
	5		9					
8						4		6
				8	4			

	2	3			8		6	
	7	4	6			9		
			9					7
		2	5			3		
	3						1	
		6			1	4		
3					5			
		1			9	6	3	
	9		4			8	2	

		4		6				
	1	6	9			3		4
3			2					
	9	7						
6	2						4	8
						7	3	
					3			5
1		2			7	8	9	
				2		6		

					7			
	2	1					4	
		4		2		7	3	5
	7		9		5			
		5				9		
			3		6		1	
2	1	9		5		8		
	6					2	7	
			2					

					9			
1	8						5	3
5	7	6				9		1
		7		9				
8								4
				5		6		
3		5				7	1	8
7	4						3	9
			8					

Puzzle 219

4				9		3		
					2	6		
			8			9	2	
				7		1		5
			2		3			
8		9		5				
	5	2			6			
		1	7					
		3		4				7

Puzzle 220

		6						3
			9		3	5		
2	1		6		5			
8	5						2	
			2		7			
	3						4	6
			3		6		1	4
		1	4		8			
6						8		

221

		3			9			
7					1		2	
	4		7				8	
1		2	9			6		
				5				
		9			6	7		8
	3				5		9	
	7		6					3
			2			4		

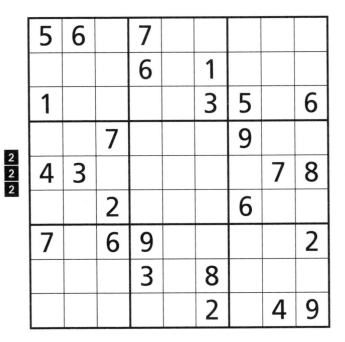

222

5	6		7					
			6		1			
1					3	5		6
		7				9		
4	3						7	8
		2				6		
7		6	9					2
			3		8			
					2		4	9

7	6			4			8	
					9		4	7
3					8	9		
		2				6		
6	5			7			3	9
		7				8		
		4	6					3
2	9		1					
	7			9			1	6

3	7							
8		5			4	3		
	2				3			8
		2	9	6			3	
	9			4			8	
	5			8	2	1		
2			8				1	
		7	2			8		5
							7	3

	4							2
		5			4		7	9
	3		9			4		
				9	8		6	
3			4		7			5
	6		3	2				
		9			2		8	
1	8		7			2		
4							1	

4	7		2		1			
1								8
		3					7	1
				6	9	3		
		6	7		5	8		
		9	4	1				
5	2					6		
9								5
			5		7		4	3

			6		9			5
3		6	1		8			4
8		1						
9	2		5		1			
				4				
			9		7		2	3
						7		6
6			7		5	4		1
1			4		6			

		8	2	7			9	
		9		4			1	2
						6		
6		5		8				
		4	3		6	5		
			5			2		8
		1						
4	2			6		9		
	5			2	9	4		

	1			4	2		9	
			3			2	1	
9				1			3	7
	9		8					
6				7				8
					1		6	
3	6			8				4
	4	5			3			
	8		4	6			2	

		1			5		3	
	8				3		7	
6				2		8		
					8	9	2	
	6						4	
	4	2	9					
		9		3				4
	5		8				1	
	3		4			7		

	8	3						
		4	6			2		
6				1	8	4	3	
			1	3		8		
1								7
		7		2	6			
	6	1	9	5				8
		8			4	1		
						9	2	

		7	1	8	9			5
1			4					
	2		7				8	
	4						5	
		9				4		
	7						3	
	9				5		6	
					8			2
3			9	6	1	8		

			8				3	
4		3						
			3		6	7	9	2
		8			2		6	
2								7
	6		1			5		
1	3	2	6		5			
						2		3
	5				7			

	2	6			7			
1			4		2			
			8			3		
		1		5		4		
	7	2				3	9	
		4		9		5		
	1			4				
			8		1			2
			5			1	4	

Puzzle 235

			6		8	9		3
					3	7		
2	3	4	5					
	4		1				3	6
9	1				4		7	
					6	1	8	7
		1	7					
5		8	3		1			

Puzzle 236

6	1							
			8				6	
		5			7			
	5		4		2	6		
3	2			5			4	1
		8	9		3		7	
			7			4		
	3				9			
							3	2

237

Puzzle 1:

		4		2				
			8			3	9	
7	5			6				
	8	1	2				6	
	7				3	8	1	
				1			3	5
	9	2			7			
				4		6		

238

Puzzle 2:

3		6	9			2		
			8		5			7
5		1						
6			2			9		
	9			1			8	
		7			9			4
						4		9
1			7		8			
		9			3	5		8

				3		5		4
4	2						9	
					9		8	
		5	1	7		6	4	
	3	1		8	6	9		
	5		8					
	1						5	7
9		6		2				

	5							
7			9				8	1
						4	9	2
			3		2		6	
		6	4		8	9		
	3		7		6			
8	1	3						
5	4				9			7
							1	

		2	3	4				9
	9	4			7	3		
			6		9		5	
1						2		
	5	9				6	8	
		3						1
	4		7		6			
		5	4			8	7	
7				8	3	4		

								1
	3	4				2		
			6		5	4	7	
	8			1				3
9			4		6			7
4				7			5	
	1	6	2		7			
		9				5	2	
8								

					4	1	9	
		4				6		
			6	2	8			3
4		9			2	3		
	3						6	
		7	3			2		8
9			2	4	7			
		3				9		
	6	2	9					

	2			4		7		
1				6				
	6	5			7			
8	4		1				9	
		2	8		9	6		
	7				3		8	2
			5			2	3	
			9					5
		1	3				7	

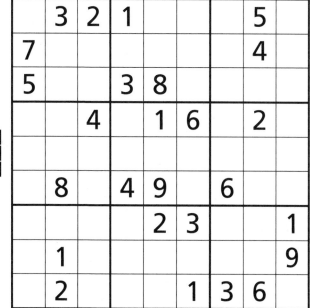

Puzzle 245:

3				7	2			
			5		1	4		
		2						3
1					3			2
	7						4	
5			4					8
6						9		
		7	2		6			
			1	4				7

Puzzle 246:

	3	2	1				5	
7							4	
5			3	8				
		4		1	6		2	
	8		4	9		6		
			2	3				1
	1							9
	2				1	3	6	

247

				9	1		5	
			8			2		6
	4							
	5	4		6		1		
	1	6	2		9	3	4	
		9		1		7	6	
							2	
3		7		4				
	6		1	2				

248

					9			2
		1			7	8		6
					8		9	3
7		2						
3	9			5			2	4
						9		5
5	2		1					
1		9	8			4		
4			6					

249

		9			5		2	
4	3			9				6
		7		1				
		3		8				
2	6						3	7
			6			8		
				5		6		
8				2			4	9
	1		6			5		

250

			9			3	4	6
8			2		6		9	1
			6			1		
6	3			5			2	8
		5			8			
2	5		4		1			3
1	7	4			9			

251

4	2		8			3		
				2			8	
			1				4	5
5	4	8						3
3						8	7	9
1	8				6			
	7			9				
		4			5		6	2

252

	9			4				
					6			1
			7		1	2		
	4	1						3
6	7						9	2
3						5	6	
		2	5		4			
9			6					
				3			4	

253

		8			6			
2	1		5					
	5	6	8				9	
3	7		9				5	1
6	9				3		2	4
	2				9	5	1	
					2		7	3
			6			2		

254

					7	1		3
	7						6	5
	5	9	6					
7	2				4			6
			1		2			
1			9				5	7
					8	6	2	
9	8						4	
6		7	2					

255

256

132

					4			8
7		8	2		6			5
	6		8				7	
2	7			6				
			3		2			
				8			9	2
	9				7		5	
3			5		8	4		7
5			4					

1		5	7	3				2
	8						3	
	2		5			1		
			3	2	7			4
		2				3		
3			8	4	9			
		1			5		9	
	7						5	
5				7	6	4		8

6		3	9	5				
	5			6				
	8				7		6	
8						3		
	7		5		4		2	
		6						7
	4		7				1	
				4			3	
				9	1	2		6

	5	2			6			
	6		9					2
3					1		7	6
				9				7
5	3						1	4
4				1				
2	4		1					5
1					3		6	
			4			8	2	

261

				3				
		7	6	4				8
					8	1	7	
	7		8		6		4	
	8			1			9	
	1		9		7		5	
	4	2	1					
8				6	4	9		
				7				

262

8		5				6		
	3			4		8	7	
		2	9	8				
	7						9	
		3	4		8	7		
	8						3	
			1	3	9			
	9	8		5			1	
		7				3		2

1				5			3	
5					6			
6	7	8				4		
2		4	1					
	1						9	
					5	1		8
		9				6	1	4
			7					3
	8			1				9

	3			7	9	4	6	
	8			5		9		
			3		2			
	9	1					4	
3								7
	2					1	3	
			6		8			
		8		2			9	
	1	9	5	4			2	

		5						7
			7			2	3	1
	1				2	9		
	3	9			1		7	8
1	5		8			3	4	
		1	2				9	
3	4	7			9			
5						6		

		8		4		9		
			2		9		3	
			6			2	8	1
						7	2	
	7			9			6	
	6	1						
8	5	4			1			
	2		8		4			
		7		2		8		

267

			8		2		6	1
	5		9			7	8	
				4			3	
			5	7	3	1		
	2	1	4	8				
	9			2				
	6	2			1		4	
4	3		6		8			

268

			3	2	9	7		
		4			7			1
2				1			5	
						1	7	
	6						9	
	1	2						
	7			4				2
3			9			8		
		8	2	6	5			

Puzzle 269

			7		1		2	
		3	6					5
		8					3	9
					6			
9				4				8
			5					
8	3					2		
5					8	1		
	7		4		2			

Puzzle 270

				3				
			2				5	6
				1	4	2		9
	1		5			6		
9				7				3
		7			1		9	
2		9	8	6				
8	6				2			
				5				

271

		6		2				
8	3	1	7					
5		2		6	8	9		
6								4
			3	8	5			
3								9
		7	8	9		4		3
					4	8	7	2
				3		6		

272

			3				2	4
	7			4		6		
		4			8		3	7
	8			3			4	
6								1
	3			2			7	
9	1		4			7		
		6		7			8	
7	2			3				

9	1		2					
5				9				
	3	4			8	1		
		9		7	5			
2								4
			6	4		5		
		6	3			2	8	
				8				5
					6		7	3

9	7	2	6			3		
1				4	3			
		4		5				2
4	5					1		
				3				
		1					9	7
6				9		4		
			1	6				9
		9			5	7	6	1

9			6					
	8	4				6	5	
		6			8			1
2				7			1	
			8		1			
	1			9				7
8			1			7		
	6	3				9	4	
					6			2

2		5						
8	1		4	6				
7					9		1	
	2	4	3					5
	7			9			4	
3					5	7	8	
	8		7					3
				8	4		7	1
						6		8

	7	4		8				9
						1	2	
9		1	5					
		5	4				9	1
3								7
4	6				7	3		
				7		2		3
	4	7						
5				1		9	7	

3					2	6		1
		9					7	3
					5	9		
	8			5	6			
			2	4			6	
		8	3					
9	3					1		
7		1	9					2

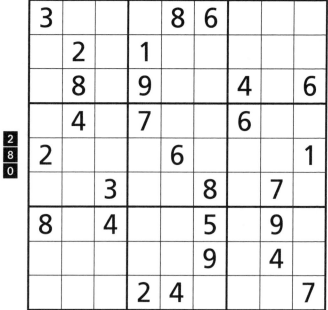

279

5	2						6	
7				4	2			
					1	5		2
		5		2			3	
	3		9		6		2	
	6			3		9		
3		8	2					
			8	1			7	
	1						9	8

280

3				8	6			
	2		1					
	8		9			4		6
	4		7			6		
2				6				1
		3			8		7	
8		4			5		9	
					9		4	
			2	4				7

						4		1
4	8	1			3		6	
					5			
			2		7		8	
7				3				2
	5		8		6			
			7					
	6		4			7	1	8
1		2						

4	1		8		7			
	3	9		2				
					1			7
	5					9		
			3	5	9			
		2					8	
8			4					
				9		8	6	
			7		2		1	9

			5			6		
					7	5	2	3
			3	8				1
			6			9	8	
3								2
	2	8			4			
2				6	8			
4	8	6	7					
		9			1			

				1				7
	1	5		3			4	
						1		8
9		1	2				7	
4	5		3		9		1	6
	3				4	8		5
1		7						
	4			8		5	3	
5				2				

	7			3				
1				4	7	2		
		9	1			6	4	
								7
	1	2	6		4	8	5	
	8							
	4	7			1	3		
		8	7	6				4
			9			2		

		3			2	8		
			9		5			
	7	2		3				4
8	6							
7			1	2	6			9
							5	6
4				8		5	6	
			3		4			
		7	5			2		

		3			5			
		7	2				9	
	5	2	8					1
4	6					7		
				3				
		9					5	4
8					4	1	2	
	2				9	6		
			5			8		

				2	9	4		
6			1				5	
3	4		7	6			9	
						2		
9	5						7	3
		8						
	6			1	7		2	4
	1				2			5
		9	6	4				

		7	4			3	1	
				3				
		4					8	2
2	7		5					
		8	7		3	6		
					9		4	3
7	8					1		
				9				
	6	1			8	2		

		9	5					
	3					7	4	
7			3	2		5		8
				9			5	6
		8				1		
9	7			6				
6		7		4	5			1
	5	1					6	
					1	4		

293

9					1	8		
	6		2				7	
					8		3	5
	3	7		2				
8				5				2
				6		8	4	
4	7		9					
	8				7		1	
	1		5					7

294

1				5			7	
	6	2						
	7		9	6		8		
		4			3			
	9	7				2	8	
			5			7		
		1		2	6		3	
						9	2	
	2			1				7

4		9		2				
							5	
	1	2	3	7				
8					6			9
		4		9		5		
3			2					8
				3	5	8	9	
	2							
				8		1		7

5					3			
	1	4		7				5
7			8					
		9	2					6
2			7	5	9			1
3					4	2		
					7			4
6				4		9	5	
			5					7

Puzzle 297:

		3	1		7		2	8
4			3					
2	8		5					
5	2					6		
3	1						8	2
	6						1	7
				9			4	1
				2				3
1	4		7		3	8		

Puzzle 298:

					9			6
			4			3		
8	2	1						
	4		2	8				
9		5		4		8		2
				3	7		1	
						5	2	3
		8			1			
7			6					

	6			5	2	1	8	
			9					
		5		8		9		6
	7		8				6	2
				3				
3	8				5		7	
8		2		1		6		
					3			
	1	3	6	4			9	

			8	3				1
	9	3	7			8		5
	1							
		4						2
		6	1		4	9		
9						5		
							9	
6		9			1	2	3	
7				4	6			

1

1	9	8	4	6	5	7	2	3
3	2	4	8	1	7	6	9	5
7	6	5	9	3	2	1	8	4
2	8	7	3	5	1	4	6	9
9	3	1	2	4	6	5	7	8
5	4	6	7	9	8	2	3	1
6	5	9	1	7	3	8	4	2
4	7	2	5	8	9	3	1	6
8	1	3	6	2	4	9	5	7

2

7	5	1	4	6	3	8	2	9
2	4	8	1	5	9	6	3	7
6	3	9	8	2	7	4	1	5
9	2	7	6	4	1	3	5	8
5	6	4	9	3	8	2	7	1
8	1	3	2	7	5	9	6	4
1	9	2	7	8	6	5	4	3
3	7	6	5	9	4	1	8	2
4	8	5	3	1	2	7	9	6

3

8	2	4	5	1	7	3	9	6
9	6	1	8	2	3	4	7	5
5	7	3	9	4	6	1	2	8
7	1	5	6	3	8	2	4	9
3	4	6	2	7	9	8	5	1
2	9	8	4	5	1	6	3	7
6	5	7	3	8	2	9	1	4
4	3	9	1	6	5	7	8	2
1	8	2	7	9	4	5	6	3

4

4	9	3	7	6	8	5	1	2
5	1	7	9	3	2	8	6	4
8	6	2	4	5	1	3	7	9
1	5	4	6	2	3	9	8	7
7	3	6	5	8	9	2	4	1
2	8	9	1	4	7	6	5	3
6	2	5	3	7	4	1	9	8
9	4	8	2	1	5	7	3	6
3	7	1	8	9	6	4	2	5

5

4	3	2	6	7	1	9	8	5
5	8	9	2	4	3	6	1	7
1	7	6	8	9	5	3	4	2
8	2	1	5	3	4	7	9	6
9	5	3	7	1	6	4	2	8
6	4	7	9	8	2	1	5	3
2	6	4	1	5	7	8	3	9
7	1	8	3	2	9	5	6	4
3	9	5	4	6	8	2	7	1

6

4	3	8	1	6	7	2	5	9
1	7	9	2	4	5	6	3	8
5	6	2	3	9	8	7	1	4
8	5	1	4	2	3	9	7	6
3	9	4	6	7	1	8	2	5
7	2	6	5	8	9	3	4	1
2	4	5	8	3	6	1	9	7
6	1	7	9	5	2	4	8	3
9	8	3	7	1	4	5	6	2

7

8	2	9	6	1	7	5	3	4
4	5	3	9	2	8	6	1	7
6	7	1	3	4	5	9	8	2
5	9	2	1	3	4	8	7	6
7	3	8	5	6	9	2	4	1
1	6	4	8	7	2	3	5	9
9	8	7	4	5	6	1	2	3
2	1	6	7	8	3	4	9	5
3	4	5	2	9	1	7	6	8

8

2	5	6	3	9	8	4	1	7
8	1	4	5	2	7	6	9	3
9	7	3	1	4	6	5	2	8
5	6	2	4	7	3	9	8	1
3	9	1	2	8	5	7	4	6
4	8	7	6	1	9	3	5	2
7	2	9	8	3	4	1	6	5
6	4	8	7	5	1	2	3	9
1	3	5	9	6	2	8	7	4

9

4	2	9	1	3	8	6	5	7
3	5	7	2	9	6	8	4	1
1	6	8	7	4	5	9	2	3
8	3	1	4	6	7	2	9	5
9	4	6	3	5	2	1	7	8
2	7	5	8	1	9	4	3	6
7	1	2	9	8	3	5	6	4
6	8	3	5	2	4	7	1	9
5	9	4	6	7	1	3	8	2

10

2	4	3	5	6	9	7	8	1
9	6	5	1	7	8	4	2	3
7	1	8	3	2	4	9	6	5
5	3	7	4	8	1	2	9	6
4	8	6	2	9	3	1	5	7
1	2	9	7	5	6	3	4	8
8	7	2	9	1	5	6	3	4
6	9	4	8	3	7	5	1	2
3	5	1	6	4	2	8	7	9

11

3	7	6	9	2	4	8	5	1
1	4	8	5	3	7	6	2	9
9	2	5	6	1	8	4	7	3
7	5	2	3	4	9	1	8	6
4	9	1	8	5	6	2	3	7
6	8	3	2	7	1	9	4	5
5	1	4	7	9	2	3	6	8
8	3	9	4	6	5	7	1	2
2	6	7	1	8	3	5	9	4

12

2	3	5	7	8	4	9	6	1
9	6	4	5	2	1	8	3	7
8	1	7	6	9	3	5	4	2
4	2	8	3	7	5	6	1	9
6	5	3	1	4	9	2	7	8
1	7	9	8	6	2	3	5	4
7	4	6	2	3	8	1	9	5
3	8	1	9	5	7	4	2	6
5	9	2	4	1	6	7	8	3

13

8	9	1	6	2	4	7	5	3
4	7	6	9	3	5	1	8	2
5	3	2	1	8	7	9	6	4
9	5	3	2	6	8	4	1	7
7	2	8	4	9	1	6	3	5
6	1	4	5	7	3	2	9	8
1	8	5	7	4	9	3	2	6
2	4	9	3	5	6	8	7	1
3	6	7	8	1	2	5	4	9

14

7	8	4	2	6	9	1	5	3
2	3	1	5	7	4	9	8	6
9	6	5	3	1	8	7	4	2
4	2	6	8	3	1	5	9	7
3	7	9	6	4	5	2	1	8
5	1	8	9	2	7	3	6	4
1	4	3	7	9	6	8	2	5
6	5	2	1	8	3	4	7	9
8	9	7	4	5	2	6	3	1

15

2	8	9	5	4	7	6	1	3
1	3	4	9	2	6	7	5	8
5	6	7	3	8	1	2	9	4
4	5	8	1	7	3	9	6	2
3	1	6	8	9	2	5	4	7
7	9	2	6	5	4	3	8	1
6	2	5	7	1	8	4	3	9
9	7	1	4	3	5	8	2	6
8	4	3	2	6	9	1	7	5

16

3	8	1	6	9	7	5	4	2
9	7	4	2	1	5	8	3	6
6	2	5	3	8	4	1	7	9
2	5	9	7	6	3	4	8	1
8	3	7	1	4	2	6	9	5
4	1	6	9	5	8	3	2	7
5	9	8	4	7	1	2	6	3
1	6	2	8	3	9	7	5	4
7	4	3	5	2	6	9	1	8

17

5	4	6	3	7	2	9	1	8
9	3	7	8	5	1	2	6	4
2	8	1	4	6	9	3	7	5
1	9	3	6	2	5	8	4	7
6	5	8	7	4	3	1	2	9
4	7	2	9	1	8	6	5	3
7	2	9	5	3	6	4	8	1
3	1	4	2	8	7	5	9	6
8	6	5	1	9	4	7	3	2

18

9	7	2	3	8	1	4	5	6
6	1	4	9	7	5	3	2	8
5	8	3	4	2	6	1	7	9
4	3	9	2	6	7	8	1	5
7	6	5	8	1	3	9	4	2
8	2	1	5	4	9	6	3	7
2	5	6	1	9	4	7	8	3
1	9	8	7	3	2	5	6	4
3	4	7	6	5	8	2	9	1

19

9	4	7	2	5	3	8	6	1
6	2	1	7	9	8	5	3	4
5	8	3	4	1	6	2	7	9
4	9	5	8	7	2	3	1	6
1	6	8	3	4	5	7	9	2
7	3	2	9	6	1	4	8	5
2	5	6	1	3	7	9	4	8
3	1	4	5	8	9	6	2	7
8	7	9	6	2	4	1	5	3

20

8	7	4	6	3	1	9	5	2
6	5	2	9	7	4	8	3	1
1	3	9	8	5	2	6	4	7
3	4	8	5	6	7	1	2	9
7	9	6	1	2	3	5	8	4
2	1	5	4	8	9	3	7	6
9	2	3	7	1	8	4	6	5
4	6	7	3	9	5	2	1	8
5	8	1	2	4	6	7	9	3

21

9	8	6	3	7	5	1	2	4
7	3	1	8	2	4	5	9	6
2	5	4	1	6	9	8	3	7
6	4	2	5	9	1	3	7	8
5	7	8	4	3	6	9	1	2
3	1	9	7	8	2	6	4	5
8	2	7	6	1	3	4	5	9
4	9	3	2	5	8	7	6	1
1	6	5	9	4	7	2	8	3

22

3	6	9	5	8	2	4	1	7
5	2	1	9	4	7	3	6	8
8	4	7	3	6	1	2	9	5
2	3	8	4	5	9	1	7	6
4	7	5	1	2	6	8	3	9
9	1	6	8	7	3	5	4	2
7	8	4	6	1	5	9	2	3
1	9	2	7	3	8	6	5	4
6	5	3	2	9	4	7	8	1

23

1	5	2	6	3	8	7	4	9
3	8	7	1	4	9	2	6	5
9	6	4	5	7	2	1	8	3
4	2	5	8	9	6	3	7	1
7	9	8	4	1	3	5	2	6
6	1	3	2	5	7	8	9	4
5	3	9	7	2	4	6	1	8
2	4	6	3	8	1	9	5	7
8	7	1	9	6	5	4	3	2

24

3	6	2	5	1	4	8	9	7
8	9	1	7	2	6	4	3	5
7	4	5	9	8	3	2	6	1
1	7	9	2	4	8	6	5	3
2	3	4	6	5	9	1	7	8
6	5	8	1	3	7	9	2	4
9	8	6	4	7	5	3	1	2
5	2	3	8	9	1	7	4	6
4	1	7	3	6	2	5	8	9

25

5	9	3	4	1	6	8	2	7
4	8	7	9	2	3	6	1	5
2	1	6	5	7	8	4	9	3
9	4	8	3	5	1	7	6	2
7	5	1	2	6	9	3	4	8
6	3	2	7	8	4	1	5	9
3	7	5	6	4	2	9	8	1
1	6	9	8	3	5	2	7	4
8	2	4	1	9	7	5	3	6

26

9	7	4	2	5	8	1	3	6
1	5	2	3	9	6	4	7	8
6	3	8	1	4	7	2	9	5
8	9	3	4	2	5	6	1	7
5	4	1	7	6	9	8	2	3
2	6	7	8	1	3	9	5	4
7	8	6	9	3	2	5	4	1
4	2	5	6	7	1	3	8	9
3	1	9	5	8	4	7	6	2

27

6	4	2	5	9	8	3	1	7
5	8	3	7	6	1	9	4	2
9	1	7	3	2	4	8	6	5
7	5	9	6	1	3	4	2	8
4	2	6	8	5	9	7	3	1
1	3	8	2	4	7	6	5	9
2	7	1	4	8	6	5	9	3
8	9	4	1	3	5	2	7	6
3	6	5	9	7	2	1	8	4

28

2	8	9	6	4	7	3	5	1
7	3	6	1	2	5	9	4	8
5	4	1	8	9	3	2	6	7
3	7	2	5	8	9	4	1	6
6	1	5	3	7	4	8	9	2
8	9	4	2	6	1	5	7	3
1	6	3	9	5	8	7	2	4
4	5	8	7	1	2	6	3	9
9	2	7	4	3	6	1	8	5

29

4	7	9	6	2	3	1	8	5
2	6	3	5	1	8	4	9	7
8	5	1	4	9	7	6	2	3
3	8	4	7	6	2	9	5	1
6	1	7	3	5	9	8	4	2
9	2	5	8	4	1	3	7	6
1	9	6	2	8	5	7	3	4
7	4	2	9	3	6	5	1	8
5	3	8	1	7	4	2	6	9

30

3	9	6	4	8	5	2	1	7
8	7	5	1	6	2	3	4	9
4	1	2	7	9	3	5	6	8
7	6	3	8	2	4	1	9	5
1	5	9	6	3	7	8	2	4
2	4	8	5	1	9	6	7	3
9	3	4	2	5	1	7	8	6
6	2	7	3	4	8	9	5	1
5	8	1	9	7	6	4	3	2

31

8	5	2	4	3	9	1	6	7
6	9	4	5	1	7	2	3	8
7	3	1	8	2	6	9	4	5
4	6	7	9	5	1	8	2	3
9	8	3	7	6	2	5	1	4
1	2	5	3	8	4	6	7	9
5	1	8	2	4	3	7	9	6
3	7	6	1	9	5	4	8	2
2	4	9	6	7	8	3	5	1

32

5	9	4	2	6	7	3	8	1
3	8	6	4	5	1	7	9	2
2	7	1	3	9	8	6	4	5
4	3	9	7	2	5	8	1	6
6	2	8	1	4	3	5	7	9
1	5	7	6	8	9	2	3	4
7	6	3	5	1	4	9	2	8
9	4	5	8	7	2	1	6	3
8	1	2	9	3	6	4	5	7

33

4	9	2	7	6	5	8	1	3
3	1	6	4	8	2	5	9	7
8	5	7	3	9	1	6	2	4
9	2	5	8	3	7	1	4	6
6	3	1	5	4	9	2	7	8
7	8	4	1	2	6	3	5	9
1	6	3	2	7	4	9	8	5
5	4	8	9	1	3	7	6	2
2	7	9	6	5	8	4	3	1

34

2	5	4	9	7	1	6	8	3
6	3	8	4	2	5	1	7	9
9	7	1	6	8	3	2	4	5
3	2	5	8	1	6	4	9	7
4	6	9	5	3	7	8	1	2
8	1	7	2	9	4	5	3	6
5	8	6	3	4	9	7	2	1
7	9	2	1	5	8	3	6	4
1	4	3	7	6	2	9	5	8

35

1	2	9	7	4	3	5	6	8
6	3	8	2	9	5	1	4	7
4	7	5	1	6	8	3	2	9
8	6	7	3	1	9	2	5	4
3	9	2	6	5	4	8	7	1
5	1	4	8	7	2	9	3	6
2	8	1	4	3	7	6	9	5
9	4	6	5	2	1	7	8	3
7	5	3	9	8	6	4	1	2

36

2	5	3	4	1	9	7	8	6
6	7	1	3	5	8	9	2	4
4	9	8	7	6	2	5	1	3
3	1	9	8	4	6	2	7	5
7	8	4	9	2	5	3	6	1
5	2	6	1	3	7	8	4	9
8	3	2	6	9	1	4	5	7
9	6	7	5	8	4	1	3	2
1	4	5	2	7	3	6	9	8

37

4	6	2	5	8	9	1	3	7
1	9	5	4	7	3	2	6	8
7	3	8	6	1	2	5	4	9
9	1	7	2	3	8	6	5	4
8	4	6	9	5	1	7	2	3
5	2	3	7	4	6	9	8	1
6	5	1	3	9	4	8	7	2
3	7	9	8	2	5	4	1	6
2	8	4	1	6	7	3	9	5

38

2	6	3	8	9	1	5	4	7
7	1	8	6	5	4	2	3	9
4	9	5	7	3	2	1	8	6
3	5	4	9	2	6	7	1	8
8	7	9	3	1	5	6	2	4
6	2	1	4	8	7	3	9	5
1	8	6	5	4	3	9	7	2
9	3	7	2	6	8	4	5	1
5	4	2	1	7	9	8	6	3

39

9	7	4	6	3	1	2	5	8
5	1	2	9	8	4	6	7	3
8	6	3	2	7	5	4	1	9
7	9	1	3	2	8	5	4	6
6	3	5	1	4	7	8	9	2
4	2	8	5	6	9	7	3	1
2	4	7	8	9	3	1	6	5
3	5	6	7	1	2	9	8	4
1	8	9	4	5	6	3	2	7

40

1	9	5	3	7	4	8	6	2
8	7	3	2	6	1	9	4	5
6	4	2	5	9	8	3	1	7
9	5	6	1	2	7	4	8	3
3	1	7	8	4	6	5	2	9
2	8	4	9	3	5	1	7	6
4	6	1	7	5	3	2	9	8
7	3	9	4	8	2	6	5	1
5	2	8	6	1	9	7	3	4

4-1

9	5	2	8	1	6	7	4	3
4	3	7	5	2	9	6	1	8
6	1	8	4	3	7	9	2	5
1	6	3	7	4	5	8	9	2
5	2	4	3	9	8	1	6	7
8	7	9	1	6	2	5	3	4
7	4	1	9	8	3	2	5	6
3	8	6	2	5	1	4	7	9
2	9	5	6	7	4	3	8	1

4-2

2	5	1	8	3	7	4	9	6
9	3	6	5	2	4	1	7	8
7	8	4	9	6	1	3	2	5
3	1	7	6	4	5	2	8	9
8	6	9	7	1	2	5	3	4
5	4	2	3	9	8	6	1	7
4	9	3	1	8	6	7	5	2
1	2	5	4	7	9	8	6	3
6	7	8	2	5	3	9	4	1

4-3

6	7	3	2	5	8	1	4	9
5	8	9	6	1	4	2	3	7
4	1	2	9	7	3	5	8	6
8	2	1	3	4	6	7	9	5
3	6	4	5	9	7	8	1	2
9	5	7	8	2	1	4	6	3
1	9	8	7	3	5	6	2	4
2	4	5	1	6	9	3	7	8
7	3	6	4	8	2	9	5	1

4-4

8	6	9	3	2	1	5	7	4
7	4	3	5	6	8	9	2	1
2	5	1	9	7	4	3	6	8
6	7	5	1	8	9	2	4	3
4	3	8	2	5	6	1	9	7
1	9	2	4	3	7	6	8	5
9	1	7	6	4	3	8	5	2
5	8	6	7	1	2	4	3	9
3	2	4	8	9	5	7	1	6

4-5

2	6	7	8	4	1	5	9	3
9	3	5	2	7	6	4	1	8
8	4	1	5	3	9	2	6	7
7	2	3	9	6	5	1	8	4
4	9	8	3	1	2	6	7	5
5	1	6	7	8	4	9	3	2
6	7	9	4	2	3	8	5	1
3	5	4	1	9	8	7	2	6
1	8	2	6	5	7	3	4	9

4-6

4	6	9	8	7	3	1	2	5
3	2	8	9	5	1	7	4	6
1	5	7	6	4	2	3	9	8
8	9	6	3	1	4	5	7	2
2	3	4	7	6	5	8	1	9
5	7	1	2	8	9	6	3	4
6	4	3	1	9	8	2	5	7
7	1	5	4	2	6	9	8	3
9	8	2	5	3	7	4	6	1

4-7

9	8	3	1	4	2	5	7	6
1	2	7	3	6	5	9	8	4
5	4	6	7	8	9	1	2	3
8	9	2	5	3	1	4	6	7
7	6	1	4	2	8	3	5	9
3	5	4	6	9	7	8	1	2
2	7	9	8	5	4	6	3	1
6	1	5	9	7	3	2	4	8
4	3	8	2	1	6	7	9	5

4-8

6	9	2	1	5	4	3	8	7
1	7	3	9	8	6	5	2	4
4	5	8	7	2	3	1	9	6
2	4	6	5	1	8	7	3	9
7	1	9	6	3	2	8	4	5
8	3	5	4	7	9	6	1	2
5	8	4	2	6	1	9	7	3
3	2	7	8	9	5	4	6	1
9	6	1	3	4	7	2	5	8

49

9	7	6	8	3	5	4	2	1
1	5	8	7	4	2	6	9	3
4	3	2	1	9	6	7	8	5
2	6	5	4	8	7	1	3	9
8	4	3	5	1	9	2	7	6
7	1	9	6	2	3	8	5	4
3	8	4	9	7	1	5	6	2
6	2	7	3	5	4	9	1	8
5	9	1	2	6	8	3	4	7

50

2	8	3	1	6	7	5	9	4
6	9	1	8	5	4	7	2	3
7	5	4	3	2	9	8	1	6
4	6	9	5	7	8	2	3	1
8	3	2	4	1	6	9	7	5
1	7	5	2	9	3	6	4	8
9	4	6	7	3	5	1	8	2
3	2	7	6	8	1	4	5	9
5	1	8	9	4	2	3	6	7

51

7	2	4	1	3	6	8	9	5
3	1	9	5	4	8	7	2	6
8	5	6	9	7	2	4	3	1
9	8	5	6	2	7	1	4	3
2	3	7	8	1	4	6	5	9
6	4	1	3	5	9	2	7	8
1	7	8	4	9	5	3	6	2
4	9	3	2	6	1	5	8	7
5	6	2	7	8	3	9	1	4

52

1	3	6	2	8	4	7	9	5
5	4	8	1	7	9	3	2	6
2	9	7	6	3	5	8	1	4
9	6	5	3	1	7	4	8	2
3	2	1	9	4	8	5	6	7
8	7	4	5	2	6	1	3	9
7	1	9	4	6	3	2	5	8
6	8	3	7	5	2	9	4	1
4	5	2	8	9	1	6	7	3

53

9	6	4	8	3	7	1	5	2
7	3	5	2	6	1	9	8	4
2	1	8	5	9	4	3	6	7
8	4	7	9	2	3	6	1	5
1	9	3	6	7	5	2	4	8
5	2	6	1	4	8	7	3	9
3	7	9	4	5	6	8	2	1
4	8	2	3	1	9	5	7	6
6	5	1	7	8	2	4	9	3

54

2	5	4	6	1	7	3	8	9
1	8	3	9	5	2	6	4	7
9	7	6	4	3	8	5	2	1
5	2	1	3	6	9	4	7	8
7	6	8	2	4	1	9	5	3
4	3	9	8	7	5	2	1	6
8	9	5	1	2	3	7	6	4
3	4	7	5	8	6	1	9	2
6	1	2	7	9	4	8	3	5

55

7	1	2	5	8	6	9	4	3
4	6	8	3	7	9	5	1	2
3	5	9	4	1	2	6	7	8
8	4	7	2	9	5	3	6	1
1	9	6	7	4	3	8	2	5
5	2	3	8	6	1	7	9	4
9	3	5	6	2	4	1	8	7
6	8	4	1	3	7	2	5	9
2	7	1	9	5	8	4	3	6

56

1	5	3	6	8	9	2	4	7
9	6	4	7	3	2	8	1	5
2	8	7	4	1	5	6	3	9
3	4	9	8	7	1	5	6	2
5	7	6	2	9	3	1	8	4
8	1	2	5	6	4	9	7	3
6	3	8	9	2	7	4	5	1
7	9	5	1	4	6	3	2	8
4	2	1	3	5	8	7	9	6

5 7

7	1	3	8	6	9	5	4	2
9	2	5	3	4	7	8	6	1
6	4	8	1	5	2	3	9	7
4	8	2	6	7	5	9	1	3
3	5	9	4	2	1	7	8	6
1	7	6	9	3	8	4	2	5
8	6	7	5	1	4	2	3	9
2	9	1	7	8	3	6	5	4
5	3	4	2	9	6	1	7	8

5 8

1	4	3	5	9	2	6	7	8
7	6	2	3	4	8	1	9	5
8	9	5	6	1	7	4	3	2
2	5	1	7	6	4	3	8	9
3	8	9	1	2	5	7	6	4
4	7	6	8	3	9	2	5	1
9	3	4	2	5	6	8	1	7
5	1	8	4	7	3	9	2	6
6	2	7	9	8	1	5	4	3

5 9

1	5	4	7	8	3	9	6	2
7	6	9	2	4	5	1	3	8
2	8	3	6	1	9	5	4	7
3	1	2	5	7	4	6	8	9
4	7	6	1	9	8	2	5	3
8	9	5	3	2	6	7	1	4
5	2	8	4	6	7	3	9	1
6	4	1	9	3	2	8	7	5
9	3	7	8	5	1	4	2	6

6 0

2	4	1	7	6	5	9	8	3
7	9	3	8	4	1	5	6	2
8	6	5	2	3	9	1	7	4
3	2	9	6	1	4	7	5	8
1	7	6	5	8	2	3	4	9
4	5	8	9	7	3	2	1	6
9	1	4	3	5	8	6	2	7
6	8	2	1	9	7	4	3	5
5	3	7	4	2	6	8	9	1

6 1

6	9	3	2	5	1	8	4	7
4	5	8	9	3	7	1	6	2
1	2	7	8	4	6	3	9	5
7	8	5	1	6	4	2	3	9
3	6	9	5	7	2	4	8	1
2	1	4	3	8	9	5	7	6
5	7	1	4	9	8	6	2	3
9	4	2	6	1	3	7	5	8
8	3	6	7	2	5	9	1	4

6 2

2	1	5	7	8	3	4	6	9
7	9	4	1	2	6	3	5	8
8	6	3	9	5	4	1	7	2
3	4	2	8	1	7	5	9	6
5	7	9	6	3	2	8	1	4
1	8	6	5	4	9	2	3	7
4	3	7	2	6	5	9	8	1
6	2	1	3	9	8	7	4	5
9	5	8	4	7	1	6	2	3

6 3

8	7	3	1	2	9	5	6	4
1	4	9	5	3	6	2	8	7
5	6	2	8	4	7	3	9	1
7	3	6	9	1	2	4	5	8
2	5	1	6	8	4	9	7	3
9	8	4	7	5	3	6	1	2
4	1	7	2	6	5	8	3	9
6	2	8	3	9	1	7	4	5
3	9	5	4	7	8	1	2	6

6 4

2	7	1	6	4	9	5	3	8
9	6	4	3	8	5	7	2	1
3	8	5	7	2	1	9	6	4
5	9	2	1	3	8	4	7	6
7	1	6	5	9	4	3	8	2
4	3	8	2	6	7	1	5	9
6	4	7	8	1	3	2	9	5
8	5	9	4	7	2	6	1	3
1	2	3	9	5	6	8	4	7

65

9	1	6	7	2	4	5	3	8
8	3	2	5	1	9	6	4	7
4	5	7	6	8	3	9	1	2
3	6	1	2	9	8	7	5	4
7	4	5	1	3	6	2	8	9
2	9	8	4	7	5	1	6	3
1	2	3	8	6	7	4	9	5
5	7	9	3	4	1	8	2	6
6	8	4	9	5	2	3	7	1

66

3	1	2	6	4	9	8	5	7
6	5	8	2	7	3	4	1	9
9	4	7	8	5	1	6	3	2
4	7	6	5	9	2	1	8	3
8	2	3	1	6	7	5	9	4
5	9	1	4	3	8	7	2	6
2	3	5	7	8	4	9	6	1
1	6	4	9	2	5	3	7	8
7	8	9	3	1	6	2	4	5

67

9	1	2	7	6	8	5	4	3
6	7	4	1	5	3	8	2	9
3	5	8	9	4	2	1	6	7
1	2	9	8	3	7	6	5	4
4	8	6	5	1	9	7	3	2
7	3	5	4	2	6	9	8	1
5	9	7	3	8	4	2	1	6
2	4	1	6	7	5	3	9	8
8	6	3	2	9	1	4	7	5

68

6	4	5	1	9	2	7	3	8
1	9	3	6	7	8	2	4	5
7	2	8	4	3	5	1	6	9
8	5	7	9	4	6	3	2	1
2	6	1	7	5	3	9	8	4
9	3	4	2	8	1	5	7	6
3	7	6	5	1	4	8	9	2
5	8	2	3	6	9	4	1	7
4	1	9	8	2	7	6	5	3

69

9	3	4	2	5	7	6	1	8
5	7	8	9	6	1	2	4	3
6	1	2	4	8	3	9	7	5
7	8	3	1	9	2	4	5	6
4	9	5	6	3	8	1	2	7
1	2	6	7	4	5	8	3	9
8	4	7	3	2	6	5	9	1
3	6	9	5	1	4	7	8	2
2	5	1	8	7	9	3	6	4

70

3	9	4	7	1	6	5	2	8
2	5	1	8	3	4	6	9	7
8	6	7	2	5	9	3	1	4
7	3	5	1	2	8	9	4	6
6	8	9	3	4	5	1	7	2
1	4	2	6	9	7	8	5	3
4	2	8	9	6	1	7	3	5
9	7	3	5	8	2	4	6	1
5	1	6	4	7	3	2	8	9

71

9	1	4	6	5	3	8	2	7
8	3	2	9	7	1	6	5	4
6	5	7	8	4	2	3	1	9
1	8	9	2	6	5	4	7	3
4	7	5	3	1	8	9	6	2
3	2	6	4	9	7	5	8	1
5	4	3	7	2	6	1	9	8
2	9	1	5	8	4	7	3	6
7	6	8	1	3	9	2	4	5

72

9	7	2	1	6	3	8	4	5
3	1	5	2	8	4	9	6	7
6	4	8	5	9	7	3	1	2
1	6	7	8	5	9	2	3	4
2	9	3	6	4	1	5	7	8
5	8	4	7	3	2	6	9	1
8	5	1	3	7	6	4	2	9
7	3	9	4	2	5	1	8	6
4	2	6	9	1	8	7	5	3

73

5	4	2	1	3	8	6	9	7
7	1	9	2	4	6	3	5	8
6	3	8	7	9	5	4	1	2
8	7	1	5	2	4	9	3	6
9	2	6	8	1	3	5	7	4
4	5	3	6	7	9	8	2	1
2	6	5	3	8	7	1	4	9
1	8	4	9	5	2	7	6	3
3	9	7	4	6	1	2	8	5

74

9	6	2	7	3	1	8	4	5
8	1	4	6	5	2	7	3	9
3	7	5	4	8	9	1	2	6
5	3	8	1	9	7	2	6	4
7	2	9	8	6	4	5	1	3
1	4	6	5	2	3	9	8	7
4	5	1	2	7	6	3	9	8
2	8	3	9	4	5	6	7	1
6	9	7	3	1	8	4	5	2

75

8	6	3	5	9	1	2	7	4
9	5	7	6	4	2	3	8	1
1	4	2	3	7	8	9	6	5
7	8	6	9	1	3	5	4	2
2	1	5	8	6	4	7	3	9
4	3	9	2	5	7	6	1	8
5	7	4	1	2	6	8	9	3
3	9	1	7	8	5	4	2	6
6	2	8	4	3	9	1	5	7

76

5	9	7	4	6	1	8	3	2
2	3	1	5	8	7	6	4	9
6	4	8	2	3	9	5	1	7
7	8	2	1	9	4	3	6	5
9	1	6	8	5	3	7	2	4
3	5	4	6	7	2	1	9	8
4	7	3	9	1	5	2	8	6
8	2	5	3	4	6	9	7	1
1	6	9	7	2	8	4	5	3

77

8	6	9	5	4	1	3	2	7
4	3	2	8	6	7	5	1	9
1	7	5	2	9	3	4	6	8
3	4	6	9	1	5	7	8	2
7	5	8	6	3	2	9	4	1
9	2	1	7	8	4	6	3	5
2	1	3	4	5	9	8	7	6
5	8	7	3	2	6	1	9	4
6	9	4	1	7	8	2	5	3

78

3	5	7	1	9	6	2	8	4
1	9	6	4	2	8	7	3	5
2	8	4	5	7	3	6	1	9
4	6	1	3	5	7	9	2	8
5	3	2	9	8	1	4	7	6
9	7	8	6	4	2	1	5	3
8	1	5	7	6	4	3	9	2
7	4	9	2	3	5	8	6	1
6	2	3	8	1	9	5	4	7

79

4	6	5	2	7	3	8	1	9
1	2	8	9	4	5	3	7	6
3	7	9	8	1	6	5	2	4
2	8	4	6	9	1	7	5	3
9	5	6	3	2	7	1	4	8
7	1	3	4	5	8	6	9	2
6	9	7	5	8	2	4	3	1
8	4	1	7	3	9	2	6	5
5	3	2	1	6	4	9	8	7

80

7	8	3	9	5	2	1	4	6
2	5	9	6	4	1	7	8	3
1	6	4	7	3	8	2	5	9
8	2	1	4	6	5	3	9	7
5	9	7	8	1	3	4	6	2
4	3	6	2	9	7	8	1	5
6	1	8	3	2	9	5	7	4
9	7	2	5	8	4	6	3	1
3	4	5	1	7	6	9	2	8

8-1

4	3	1	9	2	8	6	5	7
5	8	9	1	6	7	4	3	2
6	2	7	3	4	5	8	1	9
2	5	8	4	1	6	7	9	3
3	9	4	7	5	2	1	8	6
7	1	6	8	9	3	5	2	4
1	7	3	2	8	4	9	6	5
8	4	5	6	3	9	2	7	1
9	6	2	5	7	1	3	4	8

8-2

9	8	4	5	7	3	1	6	2
7	3	6	8	2	1	5	4	9
5	2	1	9	6	4	8	7	3
3	4	9	6	5	2	7	1	8
2	6	8	4	1	7	9	3	5
1	5	7	3	8	9	4	2	6
8	7	5	1	3	6	2	9	4
6	9	2	7	4	5	3	8	1
4	1	3	2	9	8	6	5	7

8-3

2	7	6	4	8	9	5	1	3
3	5	4	1	7	6	9	2	8
9	8	1	2	5	3	7	6	4
8	6	9	3	4	5	1	7	2
4	3	2	7	9	1	6	8	5
5	1	7	8	6	2	4	3	9
1	4	5	6	2	8	3	9	7
7	2	3	9	1	4	8	5	6
6	9	8	5	3	7	2	4	1

8-4

1	9	3	4	6	7	2	5	8
4	5	2	3	9	8	7	6	1
6	8	7	1	5	2	9	3	4
3	7	5	9	8	6	1	4	2
8	1	4	7	2	3	5	9	6
2	6	9	5	1	4	3	8	7
7	3	1	8	4	5	6	2	9
5	4	6	2	7	9	8	1	3
9	2	8	6	3	1	4	7	5

8-5

1	8	9	7	5	4	2	6	3
2	3	5	8	9	6	1	7	4
4	6	7	2	3	1	5	8	9
9	1	4	5	2	7	6	3	8
7	2	3	1	6	8	4	9	5
8	5	6	9	4	3	7	1	2
5	9	1	3	7	2	8	4	6
3	4	8	6	1	5	9	2	7
6	7	2	4	8	9	3	5	1

8-6

4	9	7	3	8	2	5	6	1
5	6	3	7	4	1	2	8	9
8	2	1	9	5	6	7	4	3
3	8	4	5	1	7	9	2	6
6	7	5	2	9	3	4	1	8
2	1	9	4	6	8	3	5	7
9	4	8	6	3	5	1	7	2
1	3	2	8	7	4	6	9	5
7	5	6	1	2	9	8	3	4

8-7

1	7	3	2	9	4	5	8	6
9	8	6	3	5	1	4	7	2
4	2	5	7	8	6	9	3	1
3	5	7	6	1	2	8	9	4
8	4	2	9	3	7	6	1	5
6	9	1	8	4	5	3	2	7
2	1	9	4	6	8	7	5	3
5	3	4	1	7	9	2	6	8
7	6	8	5	2	3	1	4	9

8-8

8	7	6	2	9	1	5	3	4
3	9	5	4	6	7	2	8	1
1	2	4	5	3	8	6	9	7
7	1	3	9	8	5	4	2	6
9	4	8	7	2	6	1	5	3
5	6	2	3	1	4	8	7	9
4	8	7	1	5	3	9	6	2
6	3	9	8	4	2	7	1	5
2	5	1	6	7	9	3	4	8

8	1	3	4	6	2	5	9	7
5	2	6	9	1	7	8	4	3
4	7	9	8	5	3	1	6	2
2	8	5	7	4	1	9	3	6
9	6	7	5	3	8	4	2	1
3	4	1	2	9	6	7	5	8
7	9	2	6	8	4	3	1	5
1	5	8	3	2	9	6	7	4
6	3	4	1	7	5	2	8	9

1	5	6	3	7	8	9	4	2
9	7	3	5	4	2	6	8	1
8	2	4	9	6	1	5	3	7
7	1	8	6	5	3	4	2	9
4	3	5	8	2	9	1	7	6
6	9	2	7	1	4	3	5	8
5	4	7	2	9	6	8	1	3
2	8	9	1	3	5	7	6	4
3	6	1	4	8	7	2	9	5

1	8	3	7	5	2	6	4	9
7	4	2	8	6	9	3	5	1
6	5	9	3	4	1	7	2	8
5	3	1	6	8	4	9	7	2
9	2	7	1	3	5	4	8	6
4	6	8	2	9	7	1	3	5
8	7	4	5	1	6	2	9	3
3	9	6	4	2	8	5	1	7
2	1	5	9	7	3	8	6	4

2	9	1	3	8	4	6	7	5
7	5	6	1	2	9	3	4	8
3	4	8	5	6	7	9	2	1
6	3	5	2	4	1	8	9	7
1	2	7	6	9	8	4	5	3
9	8	4	7	5	3	1	6	2
5	1	3	4	7	6	2	8	9
4	7	9	8	1	2	5	3	6
8	6	2	9	3	5	7	1	4

4	8	5	1	9	6	3	2	7
7	2	1	3	4	8	6	9	5
6	9	3	7	2	5	1	8	4
9	6	7	4	8	3	2	5	1
1	5	2	9	6	7	4	3	8
3	4	8	5	1	2	7	6	9
8	3	4	6	7	9	5	1	2
2	7	6	8	5	1	9	4	3
5	1	9	2	3	4	8	7	6

2	1	4	5	8	3	6	7	9
9	7	5	6	1	4	2	8	3
8	3	6	7	2	9	1	4	5
1	5	9	2	6	8	4	3	7
4	2	7	1	3	5	9	6	8
3	6	8	4	9	7	5	2	1
6	4	3	9	7	1	8	5	2
7	9	2	8	5	6	3	1	4
5	8	1	3	4	2	7	9	6

4	7	1	5	8	9	6	3	2
6	8	3	2	1	7	5	4	9
2	5	9	4	6	3	1	7	8
5	2	6	3	7	8	9	1	4
9	1	8	6	4	2	7	5	3
3	4	7	9	5	1	8	2	6
1	6	4	8	3	5	2	9	7
8	9	5	7	2	4	3	6	1
7	3	2	1	9	6	4	8	5

4	2	8	1	7	3	6	5	9
9	6	7	2	4	5	1	8	3
5	1	3	8	9	6	4	7	2
7	4	5	6	2	1	9	3	8
6	3	9	7	8	4	5	2	1
2	8	1	3	5	9	7	4	6
1	9	4	5	3	8	2	6	7
3	5	2	9	6	7	8	1	4
8	7	6	4	1	2	3	9	5

97

9	2	8	6	5	1	7	3	4
1	3	7	2	8	4	9	6	5
6	4	5	7	3	9	1	2	8
3	6	1	9	2	5	8	4	7
5	8	2	4	7	3	6	9	1
4	7	9	8	1	6	2	5	3
2	1	6	5	4	8	3	7	9
7	5	3	1	9	2	4	8	6
8	9	4	3	6	7	5	1	2

98

8	1	2	7	3	6	5	9	4
6	4	5	1	9	2	3	8	7
9	7	3	8	5	4	2	1	6
2	6	8	5	4	9	7	3	1
5	3	7	2	6	1	8	4	9
4	9	1	3	7	8	6	5	2
3	5	9	6	1	7	4	2	8
1	2	6	4	8	5	9	7	3
7	8	4	9	2	3	1	6	5

99

2	4	8	1	7	5	6	3	9
9	3	1	4	6	2	5	7	8
5	6	7	8	3	9	4	2	1
3	7	9	5	4	8	1	6	2
4	8	2	3	1	6	9	5	7
6	1	5	2	9	7	3	8	4
1	9	6	7	2	3	8	4	5
8	2	3	9	5	4	7	1	6
7	5	4	6	8	1	2	9	3

100

8	4	2	9	5	1	7	6	3
5	3	9	6	2	7	1	8	4
6	1	7	4	8	3	2	5	9
7	2	1	3	9	8	5	4	6
3	5	8	7	6	4	9	2	1
4	9	6	5	1	2	8	3	7
9	8	5	1	3	6	4	7	2
1	7	3	2	4	5	6	9	8
2	6	4	8	7	9	3	1	5

101

8	9	5	7	2	1	4	6	3
6	1	7	3	8	4	9	2	5
2	3	4	5	9	6	1	7	8
9	4	6	2	7	5	8	3	1
5	8	3	6	1	9	2	4	7
7	2	1	4	3	8	6	5	9
4	5	9	8	6	7	3	1	2
3	7	8	1	4	2	5	9	6
1	6	2	9	5	3	7	8	4

102

4	2	5	9	1	6	8	7	3
9	6	7	2	3	8	4	5	1
3	8	1	7	4	5	6	9	2
2	5	3	1	8	4	9	6	7
6	9	8	5	7	3	1	2	4
1	7	4	6	2	9	3	8	5
7	1	6	4	9	2	5	3	8
8	4	9	3	5	7	2	1	6
5	3	2	8	6	1	7	4	9

103

4	9	5	8	3	6	2	7	1
8	1	7	5	4	2	6	3	9
2	3	6	7	9	1	8	5	4
9	2	1	6	5	7	3	4	8
7	8	3	9	2	4	1	6	5
5	6	4	3	1	8	9	2	7
6	4	2	1	7	9	5	8	3
1	5	8	4	6	3	7	9	2
3	7	9	2	8	5	4	1	6

104

7	2	8	6	4	5	1	3	9
9	6	5	7	1	3	4	2	8
1	4	3	2	8	9	6	7	5
6	9	4	1	7	8	3	5	2
5	1	7	3	9	2	8	6	4
3	8	2	4	5	6	9	1	7
2	3	9	5	6	4	7	8	1
4	7	6	8	2	1	5	9	3
8	5	1	9	3	7	2	4	6

105

3	9	6	1	2	4	8	5	7
8	1	5	3	9	7	4	6	2
7	4	2	6	8	5	3	9	1
2	5	3	8	7	9	1	4	6
1	6	4	2	5	3	7	8	9
9	8	7	4	6	1	5	2	3
5	2	9	7	3	8	6	1	4
6	7	1	5	4	2	9	3	8
4	3	8	9	1	6	2	7	5

106

8	5	2	3	9	1	7	6	4
6	3	4	8	5	7	1	2	9
7	1	9	4	2	6	5	8	3
5	7	1	6	3	8	4	9	2
3	2	8	5	4	9	6	7	1
9	4	6	7	1	2	8	3	5
1	6	3	2	7	4	9	5	8
2	9	7	1	8	5	3	4	6
4	8	5	9	6	3	2	1	7

107

5	3	8	6	4	2	1	9	7
7	9	1	5	8	3	4	2	6
4	2	6	1	7	9	5	3	8
8	4	7	9	5	6	3	1	2
2	1	9	7	3	8	6	4	5
6	5	3	2	1	4	8	7	9
9	8	4	3	2	5	7	6	1
3	7	2	8	6	1	9	5	4
1	6	5	4	9	7	2	8	3

108

3	6	7	8	2	5	9	4	1
4	9	8	6	1	3	7	2	5
2	1	5	9	4	7	8	6	3
9	7	4	3	8	6	1	5	2
6	2	3	7	5	1	4	8	9
8	5	1	2	9	4	6	3	7
5	3	6	1	7	8	2	9	4
1	8	9	4	3	2	5	7	6
7	4	2	5	6	9	3	1	8

109

3	9	1	8	5	2	6	4	7
7	4	2	9	6	3	8	5	1
6	8	5	1	7	4	3	9	2
9	6	8	5	3	7	1	2	4
5	7	3	4	2	1	9	6	8
2	1	4	6	9	8	5	7	3
1	5	7	3	4	6	2	8	9
4	3	6	2	8	9	7	1	5
8	2	9	7	1	5	4	3	6

110

8	9	4	5	7	3	1	2	6
6	7	1	4	9	2	3	8	5
5	2	3	8	1	6	7	9	4
9	8	2	3	5	1	6	4	7
3	6	5	7	8	4	9	1	2
1	4	7	2	6	9	5	3	8
4	5	8	1	3	7	2	6	9
2	1	9	6	4	5	8	7	3
7	3	6	9	2	8	4	5	1

111

3	4	6	5	9	2	1	8	7
1	2	9	6	7	8	5	3	4
7	8	5	4	1	3	9	2	6
6	9	1	7	3	5	8	4	2
8	7	4	1	2	6	3	5	9
5	3	2	8	4	9	6	7	1
9	5	8	2	6	7	4	1	3
2	1	3	9	5	4	7	6	8
4	6	7	3	8	1	2	9	5

112

3	5	4	6	1	2	8	7	9
7	2	8	5	9	3	4	1	6
6	1	9	7	4	8	3	2	5
9	4	5	2	3	7	1	6	8
8	7	6	9	5	1	2	4	3
1	3	2	8	6	4	9	5	7
4	9	3	1	7	5	6	8	2
5	8	1	3	2	6	7	9	4
2	6	7	4	8	9	5	3	1

13

8	3	9	7	6	2	1	4	5
6	1	4	9	3	5	8	2	7
7	5	2	4	8	1	9	6	3
3	2	5	8	7	9	4	1	6
9	6	8	3	1	4	5	7	2
4	7	1	2	5	6	3	8	9
5	4	7	6	9	8	2	3	1
2	9	3	1	4	7	6	5	8
1	8	6	5	2	3	7	9	4

14

4	9	8	2	6	5	3	1	7
2	6	5	1	3	7	4	8	9
3	1	7	9	4	8	2	5	6
8	5	6	3	2	4	9	7	1
1	4	2	5	7	9	6	3	8
9	7	3	6	8	1	5	2	4
5	2	9	8	1	6	7	4	3
6	8	4	7	5	3	1	9	2
7	3	1	4	9	2	8	6	5

15

7	9	8	4	1	2	3	5	6
1	3	4	6	9	5	7	8	2
2	6	5	8	7	3	4	1	9
8	2	6	1	3	7	9	4	5
4	5	1	9	8	6	2	3	7
9	7	3	5	2	4	1	6	8
6	8	7	2	4	1	5	9	3
5	1	2	3	6	9	8	7	4
3	4	9	7	5	8	6	2	1

16

8	9	6	1	2	7	5	4	3
4	5	1	9	8	3	7	6	2
7	2	3	5	6	4	8	1	9
9	6	5	2	7	8	1	3	4
1	7	4	3	5	9	6	2	8
2	3	8	4	1	6	9	7	5
5	4	2	6	9	1	3	8	7
6	8	9	7	3	2	4	5	1
3	1	7	8	4	5	2	9	6

17

8	4	1	2	3	9	7	6	5
9	7	5	6	8	1	3	4	2
3	2	6	5	7	4	8	1	9
5	3	2	4	1	8	9	7	6
1	8	9	7	5	6	2	3	4
7	6	4	9	2	3	5	8	1
4	1	8	3	9	5	6	2	7
6	5	7	8	4	2	1	9	3
2	9	3	1	6	7	4	5	8

18

8	9	4	6	3	2	7	1	5
3	7	6	9	5	1	8	2	4
5	1	2	7	8	4	6	3	9
6	3	1	8	2	9	5	4	7
4	5	8	3	7	6	1	9	2
7	2	9	4	1	5	3	8	6
1	6	3	2	9	7	4	5	8
9	8	7	5	4	3	2	6	1
2	4	5	1	6	8	9	7	3

19

7	2	5	3	6	4	8	1	9
6	1	3	5	9	8	4	2	7
4	9	8	2	1	7	5	6	3
5	8	7	9	2	3	1	4	6
1	3	2	6	4	5	9	7	8
9	6	4	8	7	1	2	3	5
3	4	9	7	8	2	6	5	1
2	7	6	1	5	9	3	8	4
8	5	1	4	3	6	7	9	2

20

2	1	6	4	7	3	8	5	9
4	5	3	6	8	9	1	7	2
7	9	8	1	5	2	6	4	3
8	7	2	9	4	6	3	1	5
9	3	4	2	1	5	7	6	8
5	6	1	8	3	7	9	2	4
6	2	5	3	9	1	4	8	7
1	4	9	7	2	8	5	3	6
3	8	7	5	6	4	2	9	1

121

7	2	4	3	1	8	5	9	6
9	1	8	6	7	5	4	3	2
3	6	5	2	4	9	1	8	7
4	9	1	7	2	6	3	5	8
8	5	2	1	9	3	7	6	4
6	7	3	8	5	4	2	1	9
2	8	7	5	6	1	9	4	3
5	4	6	9	3	7	8	2	1
1	3	9	4	8	2	6	7	5

122

4	6	7	9	2	8	5	1	3
8	1	2	4	3	5	9	6	7
3	5	9	7	6	1	8	4	2
2	3	5	8	4	6	7	9	1
7	8	4	5	1	9	2	3	6
1	9	6	3	7	2	4	8	5
6	4	1	2	9	7	3	5	8
9	7	8	6	5	3	1	2	4
5	2	3	1	8	4	6	7	9

123

2	6	3	5	4	8	7	1	9
1	4	5	7	3	9	6	8	2
9	7	8	6	1	2	3	5	4
7	1	4	8	5	3	9	2	6
5	3	2	9	7	6	8	4	1
6	8	9	4	2	1	5	3	7
3	5	7	1	9	4	2	6	8
8	2	1	3	6	7	4	9	5
4	9	6	2	8	5	1	7	3

124

8	2	6	4	9	3	1	5	7
4	9	7	5	6	1	8	2	3
3	5	1	2	8	7	6	9	4
9	8	4	7	5	2	3	6	1
6	1	5	3	4	9	2	7	8
7	3	2	6	1	8	5	4	9
2	6	3	8	7	4	9	1	5
5	4	9	1	3	6	7	8	2
1	7	8	9	2	5	4	3	6

125

9	3	8	5	4	2	7	1	6
4	7	6	9	1	8	2	3	5
5	1	2	7	3	6	4	8	9
6	5	4	3	2	1	9	7	8
3	9	1	8	6	7	5	4	2
2	8	7	4	5	9	3	6	1
8	4	9	1	7	5	6	2	3
7	2	5	6	8	3	1	9	4
1	6	3	2	9	4	8	5	7

126

3	5	8	7	4	6	1	2	9
4	6	1	8	9	2	3	5	7
7	9	2	5	3	1	8	4	6
5	7	3	6	1	8	2	9	4
1	2	6	9	7	4	5	8	3
8	4	9	3	2	5	7	6	1
2	1	7	4	5	9	6	3	8
6	3	4	2	8	7	9	1	5
9	8	5	1	6	3	4	7	2

127

3	6	9	7	2	5	4	1	8
2	5	7	4	1	8	3	6	9
1	8	4	9	3	6	5	2	7
4	7	8	3	5	2	6	9	1
9	1	2	8	6	4	7	3	5
6	3	5	1	9	7	2	8	4
5	2	1	6	7	9	8	4	3
7	4	3	2	8	1	9	5	6
8	9	6	5	4	3	1	7	2

128

1	4	5	6	2	9	8	7	3
3	2	7	8	4	5	6	9	1
6	8	9	3	1	7	5	4	2
8	3	4	5	7	1	9	2	6
2	7	6	9	3	4	1	8	5
5	9	1	2	8	6	7	3	4
7	5	2	4	6	8	3	1	9
9	1	3	7	5	2	4	6	8
4	6	8	1	9	3	2	5	7

129

9	7	3	1	5	2	4	6	8
5	6	2	8	4	3	1	9	7
8	1	4	7	9	6	2	5	3
6	5	1	9	3	7	8	4	2
4	8	9	6	2	1	3	7	5
2	3	7	4	8	5	6	1	9
1	2	8	5	6	9	7	3	4
7	4	5	3	1	8	9	2	6
3	9	6	2	7	4	5	8	1

130

2	5	9	6	7	3	8	1	4
7	8	4	9	1	2	3	6	5
6	3	1	5	4	8	2	9	7
4	1	5	2	9	7	6	8	3
9	2	6	8	3	5	4	7	1
8	7	3	1	6	4	9	5	2
5	6	7	3	2	9	1	4	8
1	4	2	7	8	6	5	3	9
3	9	8	4	5	1	7	2	6

131

1	6	2	8	9	7	4	5	3
8	9	3	2	5	4	6	7	1
7	4	5	1	3	6	9	8	2
9	3	1	4	8	5	7	2	6
4	7	6	3	2	1	8	9	5
5	2	8	6	7	9	1	3	4
6	5	7	9	1	3	2	4	8
3	8	4	7	6	2	5	1	9
2	1	9	5	4	8	3	6	7

132

7	1	9	4	2	3	5	8	6
6	4	2	8	9	5	1	7	3
8	3	5	1	6	7	9	4	2
9	7	8	6	1	2	3	5	4
2	6	1	3	5	4	7	9	8
3	5	4	9	7	8	2	6	1
5	9	6	2	8	1	4	3	7
4	2	7	5	3	6	8	1	9
1	8	3	7	4	9	6	2	5

133

9	3	7	8	1	6	5	2	4
2	6	1	7	5	4	3	9	8
4	5	8	2	3	9	6	1	7
8	4	9	6	7	3	2	5	1
3	2	5	4	8	1	9	7	6
1	7	6	5	9	2	4	8	3
5	8	3	9	4	7	1	6	2
7	1	2	3	6	5	8	4	9
6	9	4	1	2	8	7	3	5

134

4	3	5	7	8	9	1	2	6
6	9	2	3	1	5	4	8	7
7	1	8	6	2	4	9	3	5
2	5	4	8	3	6	7	1	9
8	6	9	1	4	7	3	5	2
3	7	1	9	5	2	8	6	4
5	2	3	4	7	1	6	9	8
9	8	7	2	6	3	5	4	1
1	4	6	5	9	8	2	7	3

135

7	9	2	1	5	6	3	4	8
8	5	1	7	3	4	2	6	9
3	6	4	9	8	2	5	1	7
2	3	5	6	9	8	4	7	1
4	1	9	3	7	5	6	8	2
6	7	8	2	4	1	9	3	5
9	2	3	8	6	7	1	5	4
5	8	6	4	1	9	7	2	3
1	4	7	5	2	3	8	9	6

136

1	6	3	4	7	2	8	9	5
9	7	4	6	8	5	3	2	1
8	2	5	3	1	9	4	6	7
5	4	9	8	2	6	1	7	3
6	1	8	7	4	3	2	5	9
2	3	7	5	9	1	6	4	8
7	5	2	1	6	8	9	3	4
4	9	1	2	3	7	5	8	6
3	8	6	9	5	4	7	1	2

137

3	5	9	4	1	6	8	7	2
7	1	6	9	2	8	5	4	3
8	2	4	5	7	3	6	1	9
4	8	1	3	5	2	9	6	7
2	9	7	6	4	1	3	8	5
6	3	5	8	9	7	4	2	1
1	6	8	2	3	9	7	5	4
9	4	2	7	6	5	1	3	8
5	7	3	1	8	4	2	9	6

138

8	1	6	5	3	4	7	9	2
2	7	3	9	6	8	5	4	1
5	9	4	7	2	1	8	6	3
9	6	5	4	1	2	3	7	8
7	3	8	6	5	9	1	2	4
4	2	1	8	7	3	9	5	6
3	4	9	2	8	5	6	1	7
6	8	2	1	9	7	4	3	5
1	5	7	3	4	6	2	8	9

139

7	3	4	6	8	1	2	5	9
8	9	6	3	5	2	7	4	1
1	5	2	9	7	4	8	6	3
6	1	8	5	3	7	9	2	4
2	4	9	8	1	6	5	3	7
3	7	5	2	4	9	6	1	8
9	2	3	4	6	8	1	7	5
4	8	7	1	2	5	3	9	6
5	6	1	7	9	3	4	8	2

140

2	4	9	5	8	7	1	6	3
6	1	7	4	2	3	8	9	5
8	5	3	6	1	9	7	2	4
5	2	6	8	4	1	9	3	7
4	9	8	3	7	6	5	1	2
3	7	1	2	9	5	6	4	8
7	3	5	9	6	4	2	8	1
1	6	2	7	3	8	4	5	9
9	8	4	1	5	2	3	7	6

141

1	7	8	6	4	2	9	5	3
2	3	5	8	1	9	4	6	7
6	4	9	5	7	3	2	8	1
9	1	2	7	3	5	8	4	6
5	8	3	9	6	4	1	7	2
4	6	7	2	8	1	3	9	5
7	9	1	4	2	6	5	3	8
8	2	4	3	5	7	6	1	9
3	5	6	1	9	8	7	2	4

142

7	8	5	9	6	4	1	3	2
4	6	9	3	2	1	7	5	8
2	1	3	5	8	7	4	6	9
5	4	2	7	1	9	3	8	6
9	7	6	8	3	2	5	1	4
8	3	1	4	5	6	2	9	7
6	5	7	2	9	3	8	4	1
3	9	4	1	7	8	6	2	5
1	2	8	6	4	5	9	7	3

143

3	6	2	5	7	8	4	1	9
5	9	4	2	3	1	6	7	8
7	1	8	6	4	9	2	5	3
2	3	1	4	6	5	9	8	7
8	7	9	1	2	3	5	4	6
6	4	5	8	9	7	3	2	1
4	8	3	9	1	2	7	6	5
9	5	6	7	8	4	1	3	2
1	2	7	3	5	6	8	9	4

144

9	2	5	3	7	6	1	4	8
6	3	1	2	8	4	5	9	7
8	4	7	9	5	1	3	2	6
5	7	3	6	2	8	9	1	4
1	8	6	4	3	9	2	7	5
4	9	2	5	1	7	8	6	3
3	5	4	7	9	2	6	8	1
7	1	9	8	6	3	4	5	2
2	6	8	1	4	5	7	3	9

145

1	3	9	8	7	5	4	6	2
6	2	4	9	3	1	7	8	5
5	7	8	2	4	6	9	3	1
4	1	5	7	8	3	6	2	9
8	9	2	6	1	4	5	7	3
3	6	7	5	9	2	8	1	4
7	8	1	4	2	9	3	5	6
9	5	3	1	6	7	2	4	8
2	4	6	3	5	8	1	9	7

146

7	3	5	2	6	4	9	1	8
2	4	8	9	7	1	3	5	6
9	6	1	3	8	5	4	7	2
6	8	9	1	5	2	7	3	4
4	5	3	7	9	6	2	8	1
1	2	7	8	4	3	5	6	9
8	7	2	6	3	9	1	4	5
5	1	6	4	2	7	8	9	3
3	9	4	5	1	8	6	2	7

147

5	4	3	1	8	9	7	2	6
9	6	8	7	5	2	4	1	3
1	7	2	4	6	3	8	5	9
4	9	7	8	3	1	5	6	2
8	1	5	9	2	6	3	4	7
3	2	6	5	4	7	1	9	8
2	3	4	6	1	8	9	7	5
6	5	9	3	7	4	2	8	1
7	8	1	2	9	5	6	3	4

148

5	2	4	8	1	7	9	6	3
9	3	1	2	5	6	4	8	7
7	6	8	4	9	3	2	1	5
2	9	6	1	3	4	7	5	8
3	1	7	5	8	9	6	2	4
8	4	5	7	6	2	1	3	9
1	8	2	9	7	5	3	4	6
4	7	3	6	2	8	5	9	1
6	5	9	3	4	1	8	7	2

149

9	2	3	5	8	1	6	7	4
5	1	4	7	6	2	9	3	8
6	8	7	3	9	4	1	5	2
7	6	5	1	2	3	4	8	9
4	9	2	6	5	8	3	1	7
1	3	8	4	7	9	5	2	6
2	4	9	8	3	5	7	6	1
8	5	6	9	1	7	2	4	3
3	7	1	2	4	6	8	9	5

150

3	6	1	2	5	4	7	9	8
7	9	4	8	1	6	5	2	3
5	8	2	3	7	9	4	6	1
9	7	3	4	6	5	1	8	2
6	4	8	1	9	2	3	7	5
1	2	5	7	8	3	9	4	6
2	5	6	9	3	7	8	1	4
8	3	7	6	4	1	2	5	9
4	1	9	5	2	8	6	3	7

151

7	5	2	1	4	8	6	3	9
3	4	1	5	6	9	2	7	8
8	6	9	7	2	3	5	1	4
4	8	7	9	3	5	1	6	2
6	1	5	2	8	4	7	9	3
9	2	3	6	7	1	4	8	5
1	3	6	4	9	2	8	5	7
5	9	4	8	1	7	3	2	6
2	7	8	3	5	6	9	4	1

152

9	6	7	8	5	3	2	4	1
1	5	3	2	6	4	9	8	7
2	4	8	9	7	1	5	6	3
5	8	9	3	4	6	1	7	2
3	7	1	5	8	2	6	9	4
4	2	6	1	9	7	3	5	8
6	9	2	7	3	8	4	1	5
8	1	4	6	2	5	7	3	9
7	3	5	4	1	9	8	2	6

153

1	4	2	3	5	7	6	8	9
9	6	7	1	8	2	3	4	5
3	8	5	6	4	9	2	7	1
4	9	1	2	6	5	8	3	7
2	5	3	8	7	1	4	9	6
6	7	8	4	9	3	1	5	2
5	1	4	7	3	6	9	2	8
8	2	9	5	1	4	7	6	3
7	3	6	9	2	8	5	1	4

154

3	7	8	2	6	9	5	4	1
4	9	1	8	5	3	6	7	2
6	5	2	1	4	7	9	3	8
8	3	9	5	2	6	7	1	4
2	6	4	3	7	1	8	9	5
7	1	5	9	8	4	3	2	6
5	8	3	4	9	2	1	6	7
1	4	7	6	3	5	2	8	9
9	2	6	7	1	8	4	5	3

155

4	1	2	9	6	8	5	7	3
5	6	9	4	7	3	2	1	8
8	7	3	1	2	5	6	4	9
2	8	1	5	9	7	3	6	4
3	5	4	8	1	6	7	9	2
7	9	6	3	4	2	8	5	1
1	3	7	2	5	9	4	8	6
9	2	5	6	8	4	1	3	7
6	4	8	7	3	1	9	2	5

156

2	7	1	9	8	6	5	3	4
9	6	3	5	4	2	7	1	8
5	8	4	1	3	7	6	9	2
4	1	8	7	5	3	9	2	6
3	9	5	6	2	8	1	4	7
7	2	6	4	9	1	8	5	3
6	5	9	3	7	4	2	8	1
8	4	7	2	1	9	3	6	5
1	3	2	8	6	5	4	7	9

157

8	1	7	5	4	9	3	2	6
6	3	4	8	1	2	7	5	9
5	2	9	7	3	6	8	4	1
4	8	6	9	5	3	2	1	7
9	5	3	2	7	1	6	8	4
2	7	1	4	6	8	5	9	3
7	4	2	3	9	5	1	6	8
3	6	8	1	2	4	9	7	5
1	9	5	6	8	7	4	3	2

158

7	8	1	5	4	2	3	9	6
3	2	9	6	8	7	4	5	1
5	4	6	3	1	9	7	2	8
2	1	7	8	6	4	9	3	5
4	3	5	2	9	1	8	6	7
6	9	8	7	3	5	1	4	2
8	6	4	1	2	3	5	7	9
9	7	2	4	5	8	6	1	3
1	5	3	9	7	6	2	8	4

159

3	5	1	2	4	6	8	7	9
4	2	8	5	9	7	3	6	1
9	7	6	1	3	8	2	5	4
8	4	9	6	7	5	1	2	3
6	3	2	8	1	4	5	9	7
5	1	7	3	2	9	6	4	8
2	8	4	9	6	1	7	3	5
7	6	5	4	8	3	9	1	2
1	9	3	7	5	2	4	8	6

160

1	2	5	3	8	7	9	4	6
6	8	7	5	9	4	3	2	1
9	3	4	1	2	6	5	8	7
3	5	2	9	6	8	1	7	4
8	7	1	4	3	2	6	9	5
4	6	9	7	1	5	8	3	2
2	1	3	6	4	9	7	5	8
7	9	8	2	5	1	4	6	3
5	4	6	8	7	3	2	1	9

161

2	7	6	1	5	9	3	8	4
4	1	5	7	8	3	9	2	6
3	9	8	2	4	6	5	7	1
5	4	9	3	7	2	6	1	8
1	3	2	6	9	8	4	5	7
6	8	7	4	1	5	2	3	9
7	2	4	9	3	1	8	6	5
9	5	3	8	6	7	1	4	2
8	6	1	5	2	4	7	9	3

162

9	8	3	2	4	7	6	1	5
7	4	5	9	6	1	3	2	8
2	1	6	3	5	8	4	7	9
4	3	8	7	1	2	5	9	6
5	2	7	4	9	6	8	3	1
6	9	1	5	8	3	7	4	2
1	5	4	8	3	9	2	6	7
3	6	2	1	7	5	9	8	4
8	7	9	6	2	4	1	5	3

163

2	7	5	3	6	9	8	4	1
9	6	8	2	4	1	3	7	5
4	1	3	8	5	7	2	6	9
6	2	7	1	3	8	9	5	4
3	9	4	7	2	5	1	8	6
8	5	1	6	9	4	7	3	2
7	3	6	5	1	2	4	9	8
1	8	9	4	7	6	5	2	3
5	4	2	9	8	3	6	1	7

164

3	6	5	9	7	8	4	1	2
8	2	4	6	3	1	9	5	7
1	9	7	4	5	2	8	3	6
4	5	2	8	1	3	7	6	9
9	1	3	7	2	6	5	8	4
7	8	6	5	4	9	1	2	3
2	3	8	1	9	7	6	4	5
6	4	9	2	8	5	3	7	1
5	7	1	3	6	4	2	9	8

165

2	5	7	3	1	9	6	4	8
1	3	8	2	4	6	5	7	9
9	4	6	7	5	8	2	1	3
8	2	9	6	7	3	1	5	4
6	7	5	1	8	4	9	3	2
4	1	3	9	2	5	8	6	7
3	9	1	4	6	2	7	8	5
7	8	4	5	9	1	3	2	6
5	6	2	8	3	7	4	9	1

166

3	9	8	5	4	2	6	7	1
2	6	5	9	1	7	8	3	4
7	4	1	8	3	6	2	5	9
4	1	9	2	6	5	7	8	3
5	8	7	4	9	3	1	6	2
6	2	3	7	8	1	4	9	5
8	3	2	6	5	4	9	1	7
9	5	4	1	7	8	3	2	6
1	7	6	3	2	9	5	4	8

167

8	4	7	9	1	5	3	6	2
9	3	2	4	7	6	5	1	8
6	5	1	2	3	8	9	7	4
2	6	8	1	4	3	7	5	9
5	1	3	8	9	7	4	2	6
7	9	4	6	5	2	8	3	1
1	7	9	3	2	4	6	8	5
4	8	5	7	6	1	2	9	3
3	2	6	5	8	9	1	4	7

168

2	8	1	3	6	9	4	7	5
5	4	6	1	7	8	3	2	9
3	9	7	2	5	4	8	1	6
9	2	4	8	3	1	5	6	7
1	3	5	7	9	6	2	4	8
6	7	8	5	4	2	1	9	3
8	5	9	4	2	7	6	3	1
7	1	2	6	8	3	9	5	4
4	6	3	9	1	5	7	8	2

169

6	3	7	2	8	1	9	5	4
4	1	5	9	3	6	7	8	2
9	2	8	5	7	4	6	3	1
3	7	2	6	4	5	8	1	9
8	9	1	3	2	7	5	4	6
5	6	4	1	9	8	2	7	3
2	5	6	8	1	3	4	9	7
1	4	9	7	5	2	3	6	8
7	8	3	4	6	9	1	2	5

170

8	9	5	2	4	1	6	7	3
1	6	3	7	5	8	9	2	4
4	7	2	9	6	3	1	5	8
7	4	1	5	9	2	8	3	6
9	2	8	3	7	6	4	1	5
3	5	6	8	1	4	7	9	2
6	1	7	4	2	5	3	8	9
2	3	4	1	8	9	5	6	7
5	8	9	6	3	7	2	4	1

171

6	2	5	3	7	8	9	1	4
9	4	8	6	2	1	3	7	5
7	1	3	9	5	4	6	8	2
1	5	7	8	4	3	2	9	6
8	9	6	5	1	2	7	4	3
2	3	4	7	6	9	8	5	1
4	6	9	1	3	7	5	2	8
3	8	2	4	9	5	1	6	7
5	7	1	2	8	6	4	3	9

172

2	8	4	7	6	5	1	9	3
7	3	1	2	4	9	5	6	8
5	6	9	8	1	3	2	7	4
4	9	7	3	2	1	6	8	5
3	2	6	9	5	8	4	1	7
1	5	8	4	7	6	3	2	9
6	4	3	1	8	7	9	5	2
8	1	2	5	9	4	7	3	6
9	7	5	6	3	2	8	4	1

173

9	1	5	3	4	2	8	6	7
6	2	4	8	7	5	9	1	3
8	7	3	6	9	1	4	5	2
3	8	2	1	6	4	7	9	5
1	4	7	5	8	9	2	3	6
5	6	9	7	2	3	1	8	4
2	9	1	4	3	6	5	7	8
7	5	6	2	1	8	3	4	9
4	3	8	9	5	7	6	2	1

174

9	8	6	2	4	5	3	1	7
3	1	5	9	6	7	4	8	2
4	7	2	3	1	8	6	5	9
1	4	3	8	5	2	7	9	6
5	6	9	7	3	4	8	2	1
7	2	8	1	9	6	5	4	3
2	5	4	6	7	9	1	3	8
6	9	1	4	8	3	2	7	5
8	3	7	5	2	1	9	6	4

175

5	2	7	3	1	6	8	9	4
3	8	9	5	7	4	6	2	1
4	1	6	2	9	8	7	5	3
9	5	8	1	4	2	3	6	7
1	6	4	9	3	7	5	8	2
7	3	2	8	6	5	4	1	9
6	9	1	4	8	3	2	7	5
8	4	5	7	2	1	9	3	6
2	7	3	6	5	9	1	4	8

176

8	4	6	1	3	2	7	9	5
7	2	1	4	5	9	8	3	6
3	5	9	8	6	7	1	4	2
5	7	8	2	9	1	3	6	4
9	6	3	7	4	5	2	8	1
2	1	4	6	8	3	5	7	9
6	9	7	5	2	8	4	1	3
4	8	5	3	1	6	9	2	7
1	3	2	9	7	4	6	5	8

177

2	4	5	3	6	7	1	9	8
1	8	3	2	5	9	4	7	6
9	7	6	4	1	8	3	5	2
7	6	1	5	2	3	9	8	4
4	9	8	1	7	6	5	2	3
5	3	2	9	8	4	7	6	1
6	2	4	7	9	1	8	3	5
8	1	7	6	3	5	2	4	9
3	5	9	8	4	2	6	1	7

178

3	2	7	9	4	6	8	1	5
9	4	6	1	8	5	2	7	3
5	8	1	3	7	2	6	4	9
6	7	4	5	3	1	9	2	8
1	5	2	6	9	8	4	3	7
8	9	3	4	2	7	5	6	1
4	3	5	7	6	9	1	8	2
2	6	9	8	1	3	7	5	4
7	1	8	2	5	4	3	9	6

179

9	7	4	6	8	1	2	3	5
8	6	2	7	5	3	1	4	9
5	3	1	4	9	2	6	8	7
1	9	7	2	6	4	3	5	8
6	8	5	3	7	9	4	2	1
4	2	3	5	1	8	9	7	6
7	4	9	1	2	5	8	6	3
3	5	8	9	4	6	7	1	2
2	1	6	8	3	7	5	9	4

180

7	9	5	2	6	1	3	8	4
3	2	4	9	7	8	6	1	5
1	8	6	4	5	3	2	7	9
5	4	9	1	3	2	8	6	7
2	6	7	8	4	5	9	3	1
8	1	3	7	9	6	5	4	2
9	3	8	5	1	4	7	2	6
6	7	1	3	2	9	4	5	8
4	5	2	6	8	7	1	9	3

181

3	9	7	4	5	8	2	1	6
1	8	4	7	2	6	5	9	3
5	6	2	1	3	9	7	8	4
8	5	6	2	7	1	3	4	9
7	3	9	5	6	4	8	2	1
2	4	1	9	8	3	6	5	7
4	7	5	6	9	2	1	3	8
6	1	3	8	4	5	9	7	2
9	2	8	3	1	7	4	6	5

182

2	1	4	6	9	3	8	7	5
3	8	6	2	7	5	9	1	4
7	9	5	8	4	1	6	3	2
5	7	3	1	2	8	4	6	9
9	2	8	4	3	6	7	5	1
6	4	1	9	5	7	3	2	8
4	6	9	7	1	2	5	8	3
8	3	2	5	6	4	1	9	7
1	5	7	3	8	9	2	4	6

183

6	2	8	4	1	9	3	5	7
5	1	3	6	7	8	9	4	2
9	4	7	2	3	5	1	6	8
3	8	2	1	9	6	4	7	5
4	6	5	7	8	3	2	9	1
7	9	1	5	2	4	6	8	3
2	3	9	8	6	7	5	1	4
1	7	4	9	5	2	8	3	6
8	5	6	3	4	1	7	2	9

184

1	6	8	7	3	2	4	5	9
2	4	9	5	6	8	7	3	1
5	3	7	9	4	1	2	6	8
7	5	6	3	8	4	9	1	2
9	8	2	1	5	6	3	7	4
4	1	3	2	7	9	6	8	5
3	7	4	8	9	5	1	2	6
6	2	5	4	1	3	8	9	7
8	9	1	6	2	7	5	4	3

185

3	5	8	7	4	9	2	6	1
1	4	2	8	3	6	9	5	7
6	9	7	1	5	2	4	8	3
7	3	1	4	9	8	6	2	5
5	8	6	2	7	3	1	4	9
9	2	4	5	6	1	3	7	8
2	7	5	9	1	4	8	3	6
4	1	3	6	8	5	7	9	2
8	6	9	3	2	7	5	1	4

186

1	2	3	5	4	9	6	7	8
7	6	4	3	2	8	1	5	9
8	5	9	6	1	7	4	2	3
9	7	8	4	3	1	2	6	5
6	3	2	9	7	5	8	4	1
5	4	1	2	8	6	3	9	7
3	8	6	7	9	4	5	1	2
2	9	5	1	6	3	7	8	4
4	1	7	8	5	2	9	3	6

187

5	6	4	8	2	9	7	1	3
3	2	8	1	7	5	9	4	6
7	9	1	6	3	4	8	2	5
4	1	9	7	8	3	5	6	2
2	3	7	4	5	6	1	8	9
8	5	6	2	9	1	3	7	4
9	4	2	3	1	8	6	5	7
6	8	3	5	4	7	2	9	1
1	7	5	9	6	2	4	3	8

188

2	3	8	7	5	6	1	4	9
6	5	1	9	8	4	2	3	7
9	4	7	1	2	3	6	5	8
8	6	5	3	4	7	9	2	1
3	9	4	2	6	1	8	7	5
7	1	2	5	9	8	4	6	3
5	2	6	8	3	9	7	1	4
1	8	3	4	7	2	5	9	6
4	7	9	6	1	5	3	8	2

189

5	6	2	7	1	9	3	8	4
9	4	8	6	3	5	2	7	1
1	3	7	8	4	2	6	9	5
3	5	6	4	2	7	8	1	9
8	2	4	5	9	1	7	6	3
7	1	9	3	8	6	5	4	2
6	7	3	9	5	4	1	2	8
2	9	5	1	7	8	4	3	6
4	8	1	2	6	3	9	5	7

190

6	2	8	3	1	5	9	7	4
1	9	5	6	7	4	8	3	2
7	3	4	8	2	9	5	1	6
3	1	6	5	4	2	7	9	8
5	7	9	1	6	8	2	4	3
4	8	2	7	9	3	6	5	1
8	4	3	2	5	7	1	6	9
2	6	7	9	3	1	4	8	5
9	5	1	4	8	6	3	2	7

191

7	1	6	8	4	9	3	2	5
8	5	9	2	3	7	4	6	1
3	2	4	6	1	5	8	9	7
2	4	8	7	5	6	9	1	3
1	6	5	4	9	3	7	8	2
9	7	3	1	2	8	6	5	4
5	3	1	9	8	4	2	7	6
6	9	2	3	7	1	5	4	8
4	8	7	5	6	2	1	3	9

192

5	2	6	8	1	4	7	3	9
4	3	1	5	7	9	2	6	8
8	7	9	3	6	2	5	1	4
1	5	3	9	2	8	4	7	6
7	6	8	1	4	3	9	5	2
2	9	4	7	5	6	3	8	1
6	4	5	2	3	1	8	9	7
3	8	2	6	9	7	1	4	5
9	1	7	4	8	5	6	2	3

193

4	3	6	5	9	7	8	2	1
1	8	2	3	4	6	9	7	5
5	7	9	8	1	2	6	3	4
8	4	1	2	5	9	3	6	7
6	2	7	1	3	4	5	8	9
3	9	5	7	6	8	4	1	2
2	6	3	9	7	5	1	4	8
7	5	4	6	8	1	2	9	3
9	1	8	4	2	3	7	5	6

194

5	6	9	4	8	7	3	2	1
1	4	2	3	6	5	9	7	8
7	8	3	2	9	1	6	5	4
6	3	1	8	5	9	2	4	7
9	5	4	1	7	2	8	3	6
8	2	7	6	4	3	5	1	9
2	7	8	9	3	4	1	6	5
4	1	6	5	2	8	7	9	3
3	9	5	7	1	6	4	8	2

195

4	9	2	5	6	7	3	1	8
5	3	1	8	4	2	9	6	7
7	8	6	1	3	9	5	4	2
6	1	5	4	9	8	2	7	3
3	2	9	7	1	5	6	8	4
8	7	4	3	2	6	1	9	5
9	4	3	2	7	1	8	5	6
2	6	8	9	5	4	7	3	1
1	5	7	6	8	3	4	2	9

196

5	1	6	2	4	3	8	7	9
2	7	3	6	9	8	4	5	1
9	8	4	7	5	1	3	2	6
8	2	7	1	6	9	5	3	4
3	6	9	4	2	5	7	1	8
1	4	5	3	8	7	6	9	2
7	5	8	9	1	6	2	4	3
6	9	2	5	3	4	1	8	7
4	3	1	8	7	2	9	6	5

197

8	2	6	9	3	1	7	5	4
4	5	9	6	8	7	2	3	1
3	7	1	5	2	4	9	6	8
5	6	7	8	9	2	4	1	3
2	1	4	3	7	5	8	9	6
9	8	3	1	4	6	5	7	2
1	4	5	7	6	8	3	2	9
6	3	8	2	5	9	1	4	7
7	9	2	4	1	3	6	8	5

198

1	3	8	7	5	9	6	2	4
5	2	4	6	1	3	8	7	9
6	7	9	8	4	2	5	3	1
2	5	3	9	7	4	1	8	6
9	8	1	3	6	5	7	4	2
4	6	7	2	8	1	9	5	3
7	4	5	1	3	6	2	9	8
8	1	2	4	9	7	3	6	5
3	9	6	5	2	8	4	1	7

199

2	8	7	9	5	1	3	4	6
5	6	1	3	8	4	2	7	9
4	9	3	7	2	6	8	5	1
8	4	5	6	9	2	1	3	7
1	7	9	8	3	5	6	2	4
3	2	6	4	1	7	9	8	5
9	1	4	2	7	8	5	6	3
6	5	8	1	4	3	7	9	2
7	3	2	5	6	9	4	1	8

200

3	6	2	9	7	4	1	8	5
1	5	7	2	3	8	9	6	4
4	8	9	1	6	5	2	7	3
2	3	1	7	5	6	4	9	8
5	4	8	3	1	9	7	2	6
7	9	6	4	8	2	5	3	1
9	2	5	6	4	3	8	1	7
8	7	3	5	2	1	6	4	9
6	1	4	8	9	7	3	5	2

201

5	7	9	8	1	6	3	4	2
2	6	4	9	3	7	1	5	8
3	1	8	2	4	5	7	9	6
1	2	3	7	6	4	9	8	5
8	9	5	3	2	1	4	6	7
7	4	6	5	9	8	2	3	1
9	3	1	6	8	2	5	7	4
4	8	7	1	5	3	6	2	9
6	5	2	4	7	9	8	1	3

202

2	9	5	1	4	3	7	6	8
1	7	4	6	2	8	3	9	5
3	6	8	7	9	5	4	1	2
7	2	9	5	8	4	1	3	6
4	1	3	9	6	2	5	8	7
8	5	6	3	7	1	2	4	9
6	3	7	2	1	9	8	5	4
5	4	2	8	3	6	9	7	1
9	8	1	4	5	7	6	2	3

203

3	5	8	7	4	9	2	1	6
1	9	7	8	6	2	3	4	5
2	4	6	1	5	3	9	8	7
7	2	3	4	8	6	5	9	1
4	6	5	2	9	1	8	7	3
9	8	1	3	7	5	4	6	2
6	1	4	5	2	8	7	3	9
8	3	2	9	1	7	6	5	4
5	7	9	6	3	4	1	2	8

204

4	2	7	8	9	5	6	1	3
6	9	8	3	7	1	5	4	2
5	3	1	6	2	4	7	8	9
7	5	3	9	8	2	4	6	1
9	1	2	4	6	7	3	5	8
8	6	4	5	1	3	9	2	7
2	7	9	1	5	6	8	3	4
1	4	5	7	3	8	2	9	6
3	8	6	2	4	9	1	7	5

205

2	1	8	7	9	3	6	5	4
9	6	3	5	8	4	1	7	2
4	7	5	1	2	6	9	8	3
7	2	6	8	1	9	4	3	5
5	9	4	3	7	2	8	1	6
3	8	1	6	4	5	7	2	9
6	5	7	9	3	1	2	4	8
1	4	9	2	5	8	3	6	7
8	3	2	4	6	7	5	9	1

206

9	6	5	1	3	2	4	8	7
8	4	1	7	6	9	3	5	2
3	7	2	8	4	5	1	6	9
5	8	7	4	1	3	9	2	6
1	3	6	2	9	7	8	4	5
2	9	4	5	8	6	7	3	1
6	5	3	9	7	8	2	1	4
4	2	9	3	5	1	6	7	8
7	1	8	6	2	4	5	9	3

207

1	6	5	9	3	8	2	4	7
3	7	4	2	6	1	5	8	9
2	9	8	4	7	5	6	3	1
7	1	2	3	9	6	4	5	8
8	5	9	1	4	2	3	7	6
6	4	3	8	5	7	1	9	2
9	8	1	5	2	4	7	6	3
5	2	6	7	8	3	9	1	4
4	3	7	6	1	9	8	2	5

208

4	5	1	6	3	7	9	8	2
2	8	3	5	9	4	1	7	6
9	7	6	8	2	1	5	4	3
7	9	4	3	1	5	6	2	8
6	2	5	4	8	9	3	1	7
1	3	8	7	6	2	4	5	9
8	4	2	9	5	6	7	3	1
3	6	7	1	4	8	2	9	5
5	1	9	2	7	3	8	6	4

209

4	2	6	5	7	8	1	3	9
7	5	1	2	3	9	8	6	4
3	9	8	4	6	1	2	5	7
6	4	3	1	9	5	7	2	8
1	7	2	8	4	3	5	9	6
9	8	5	6	2	7	4	1	3
8	1	7	3	5	6	9	4	2
5	3	4	9	8	2	6	7	1
2	6	9	7	1	4	3	8	5

210

8	4	5	2	3	1	6	7	9
2	1	9	8	7	6	5	4	3
3	7	6	9	5	4	8	2	1
7	3	4	1	2	5	9	8	6
9	6	1	3	4	8	7	5	2
5	2	8	6	9	7	1	3	4
4	8	3	5	1	9	2	6	7
6	9	2	7	8	3	4	1	5
1	5	7	4	6	2	3	9	8

211

3	7	8	2	6	4	1	9	5
2	5	4	8	1	9	6	7	3
9	6	1	7	3	5	4	8	2
6	3	9	4	7	2	8	5	1
4	2	5	9	8	1	7	3	6
1	8	7	3	5	6	2	4	9
7	9	6	5	2	8	3	1	4
5	1	3	6	4	7	9	2	8
8	4	2	1	9	3	5	6	7

212

5	7	4	1	2	8	9	3	6
3	6	1	9	4	5	7	2	8
8	9	2	7	3	6	4	5	1
9	4	6	2	7	1	3	8	5
7	5	3	8	6	4	2	1	9
2	1	8	3	5	9	6	4	7
1	2	7	6	8	3	5	9	4
6	8	5	4	9	2	1	7	3
4	3	9	5	1	7	8	6	2

213

3	4	8	2	5	6	1	7	9
5	9	7	3	1	8	2	6	4
2	6	1	4	9	7	5	3	8
8	3	9	5	6	2	7	4	1
1	5	2	8	7	4	6	9	3
4	7	6	9	3	1	8	5	2
6	1	3	7	2	9	4	8	5
7	8	5	1	4	3	9	2	6
9	2	4	6	8	5	3	1	7

214

1	3	6	5	7	2	9	4	8
2	7	8	6	4	9	5	1	3
5	4	9	8	3	1	2	6	7
3	8	7	4	6	5	1	2	9
4	1	2	3	9	8	6	7	5
9	6	5	1	2	7	3	8	4
7	5	4	9	1	6	8	3	2
8	2	1	7	5	3	4	9	6
6	9	3	2	8	4	7	5	1

215

9	2	3	7	5	8	1	6	4
8	7	4	6	1	2	9	5	3
6	1	5	9	4	3	2	8	7
1	8	2	5	9	4	3	7	6
4	3	9	2	6	7	5	1	8
7	5	6	3	8	1	4	9	2
3	6	8	1	2	5	7	4	9
2	4	1	8	7	9	6	3	5
5	9	7	4	3	6	8	2	1

216

9	7	4	3	6	1	5	8	2
2	1	6	9	5	8	3	7	4
3	8	5	2	7	4	1	6	9
8	9	7	4	3	6	2	5	1
6	2	3	7	1	5	9	4	8
5	4	1	8	9	2	7	3	6
7	6	9	1	8	3	4	2	5
1	5	2	6	4	7	8	9	3
4	3	8	5	2	9	6	1	7

217

3	5	8	6	4	7	1	9	2
7	2	1	5	3	9	6	4	8
6	9	4	1	2	8	7	3	5
8	7	6	9	1	5	4	2	3
1	3	5	4	7	2	9	8	6
9	4	2	3	8	6	5	1	7
2	1	9	7	5	3	8	6	4
5	6	3	8	9	4	2	7	1
4	8	7	2	6	1	3	5	9

218

4	2	3	5	1	9	8	6	7
1	8	9	7	2	6	4	5	3
5	7	6	4	8	3	9	2	1
6	3	7	2	9	4	1	8	5
8	5	2	6	7	1	3	9	4
9	1	4	3	5	8	6	7	2
3	6	5	9	4	2	7	1	8
7	4	8	1	6	5	2	3	9
2	9	1	8	3	7	5	4	6

219

4	2	6	1	9	7	3	5	8
1	9	8	5	3	2	6	7	4
3	7	5	8	6	4	9	2	1
2	3	4	6	7	9	1	8	5
5	1	7	2	8	3	4	9	6
8	6	9	4	5	1	7	3	2
7	5	2	3	1	6	8	4	9
9	4	1	7	2	8	5	6	3
6	8	3	9	4	5	2	1	7

220

5	9	6	8	4	1	2	7	3
4	8	7	9	2	3	5	6	1
2	1	3	6	7	5	4	9	8
8	5	9	1	6	4	3	2	7
1	6	4	2	3	7	9	8	5
7	3	2	5	8	9	1	4	6
9	2	8	3	5	6	7	1	4
3	7	1	4	9	8	6	5	2
6	4	5	7	1	2	8	3	9

221

6	2	3	5	8	9	1	7	4
7	9	8	3	4	1	5	2	6
5	4	1	7	6	2	3	8	9
1	8	2	9	3	7	6	4	5
3	6	7	8	5	4	9	1	2
4	5	9	1	2	6	7	3	8
2	3	6	4	7	5	8	9	1
9	7	4	6	1	8	2	5	3
8	1	5	2	9	3	4	6	7

222

5	6	8	7	2	9	4	1	3
2	4	3	6	5	1	8	9	7
1	7	9	8	4	3	5	2	6
6	1	7	2	8	5	9	3	4
4	3	5	1	9	6	2	7	8
8	9	2	4	3	7	6	5	1
7	5	6	9	1	4	3	8	2
9	2	4	3	7	8	1	6	5
3	8	1	5	6	2	7	4	9

223

7	6	9	2	4	3	5	8	1
8	2	1	5	6	9	3	4	7
3	4	5	7	1	8	9	6	2
4	3	2	9	8	1	6	7	5
6	5	8	4	7	2	1	3	9
9	1	7	3	5	6	8	2	4
1	8	4	6	2	5	7	9	3
2	9	6	1	3	7	4	5	8
5	7	3	8	9	4	2	1	6

224

3	7	6	5	2	8	9	4	1
8	1	5	6	9	4	3	2	7
9	2	4	1	7	3	6	5	8
7	8	2	9	6	1	5	3	4
6	9	1	3	4	5	7	8	2
4	5	3	7	8	2	1	6	9
2	3	9	8	5	7	4	1	6
1	4	7	2	3	6	8	9	5
5	6	8	4	1	9	2	7	3

225

9	4	6	8	7	5	1	3	2
8	1	5	2	3	4	6	7	9
2	3	7	9	1	6	4	5	8
7	2	4	5	9	8	3	6	1
3	9	1	4	6	7	8	2	5
5	6	8	3	2	1	7	9	4
6	7	9	1	4	2	5	8	3
1	8	3	7	5	9	2	4	6
4	5	2	6	8	3	9	1	7

226

4	7	8	2	5	1	9	3	6
1	9	5	3	7	6	4	2	8
2	6	3	9	8	4	5	7	1
7	1	2	8	6	9	3	5	4
3	4	6	7	2	5	8	1	9
8	5	9	4	1	3	7	6	2
5	2	4	1	3	8	6	9	7
9	3	7	6	4	2	1	8	5
6	8	1	5	9	7	2	4	3

227

2	7	4	6	3	9	1	8	5
3	9	6	1	5	8	2	7	4
8	5	1	2	7	4	3	6	9
9	2	3	5	8	1	6	4	7
7	6	5	3	4	2	9	1	8
4	1	8	9	6	7	5	2	3
5	4	2	8	1	3	7	9	6
6	8	9	7	2	5	4	3	1
1	3	7	4	9	6	8	5	2

228

5	6	8	2	7	1	3	9	4
7	3	9	6	4	5	8	1	2
1	4	2	8	9	3	6	5	7
6	7	5	9	8	2	1	4	3
2	8	4	3	1	6	5	7	9
9	1	3	4	5	7	2	6	8
8	9	1	5	3	4	7	2	6
4	2	7	1	6	8	9	3	5
3	5	6	7	2	9	4	8	1

229

5	1	3	7	4	2	8	9	6
4	7	6	3	9	8	2	1	5
9	2	8	6	1	5	4	3	7
2	9	7	8	5	6	3	4	1
6	3	1	2	7	4	9	5	8
8	5	4	9	3	1	7	6	2
3	6	2	5	8	9	1	7	4
7	4	5	1	2	3	6	8	9
1	8	9	4	6	7	5	2	3

230

7	2	1	6	8	5	4	3	9
5	8	4	1	9	3	6	7	2
6	9	3	7	2	4	8	5	1
1	7	5	3	4	8	9	2	6
9	6	8	5	1	2	3	4	7
3	4	2	9	7	6	1	8	5
8	1	9	2	3	7	5	6	4
4	5	7	8	6	9	2	1	3
2	3	6	4	5	1	7	9	8

231

2	8	3	4	9	5	6	7	1
5	1	4	6	7	3	2	8	9
6	7	9	2	1	8	4	3	5
4	5	6	1	3	7	8	9	2
1	3	2	8	4	9	5	6	7
8	9	7	5	2	6	3	1	4
3	6	1	9	5	2	7	4	8
9	2	8	7	6	4	1	5	3
7	4	5	3	8	1	9	2	6

232

4	3	7	1	8	9	6	2	5
1	8	5	4	2	6	9	7	3
9	2	6	7	5	3	1	8	4
8	4	3	6	1	2	7	5	9
2	6	9	5	3	7	4	1	8
5	7	1	8	9	4	2	3	6
7	9	8	2	4	5	3	6	1
6	1	4	3	7	8	5	9	2
3	5	2	9	6	1	8	4	7

233

7	2	6	8	5	9	1	3	4
4	9	3	7	2	1	6	8	5
5	8	1	3	4	6	7	9	2
9	4	8	5	7	2	3	6	1
2	1	5	9	6	3	8	4	7
3	6	7	1	8	4	5	2	9
1	3	2	6	9	5	4	7	8
6	7	9	4	1	8	2	5	3
8	5	4	2	3	7	9	1	6

234

3	2	6	9	1	7	8	5	4
1	8	5	4	3	2	6	7	9
9	4	7	6	8	5	2	3	1
8	9	1	7	5	3	4	2	6
5	7	2	1	6	4	3	9	8
6	3	4	2	9	8	5	1	7
2	1	9	3	4	6	7	8	5
4	5	3	8	7	1	9	6	2
7	6	8	5	2	9	1	4	3

235

1	5	7	6	2	8	9	4	3
8	6	9	4	1	3	7	2	5
2	3	4	5	7	9	6	1	8
7	4	2	1	9	5	8	3	6
3	8	5	2	6	7	4	9	1
9	1	6	8	3	4	5	7	2
4	2	3	9	5	6	1	8	7
6	9	1	7	8	2	3	5	4
5	7	8	3	4	1	2	6	9

236

6	1	9	3	2	4	8	5	7
2	7	3	8	9	5	1	6	4
8	4	5	1	6	7	3	2	9
9	5	1	4	7	2	6	8	3
3	2	7	6	5	8	9	4	1
4	6	8	9	1	3	2	7	5
5	8	2	7	3	1	4	9	6
7	3	6	2	4	9	5	1	8
1	9	4	5	8	6	7	3	2

237

9	3	4	7	2	1	5	8	6
1	2	6	8	5	4	3	9	7
7	5	8	3	6	9	4	2	1
3	8	1	2	7	5	9	6	4
2	4	9	1	8	6	7	5	3
6	7	5	4	9	3	8	1	2
4	6	7	9	1	8	2	3	5
5	9	2	6	3	7	1	4	8
8	1	3	5	4	2	6	7	9

238

3	8	6	9	7	1	2	4	5
9	4	2	8	3	5	1	6	7
5	7	1	6	2	4	8	9	3
6	3	8	2	4	7	9	5	1
4	9	5	3	1	6	7	8	2
2	1	7	5	8	9	6	3	4
8	6	3	1	5	2	4	7	9
1	5	4	7	9	8	3	2	6
7	2	9	4	6	3	5	1	8

239

1	6	9	2	3	8	5	7	4
4	2	8	7	5	1	3	9	6
5	7	3	6	4	9	1	8	2
8	9	5	1	7	2	6	4	3
6	4	2	3	9	5	7	1	8
7	3	1	4	8	6	9	2	5
3	5	7	8	1	4	2	6	9
2	1	4	9	6	3	8	5	7
9	8	6	5	2	7	4	3	1

240

9	5	1	8	2	4	3	7	6
7	2	4	9	6	3	5	8	1
3	6	8	5	7	1	4	9	2
4	8	9	3	1	2	7	6	5
1	7	6	4	5	8	9	2	3
2	3	5	7	9	6	1	4	8
8	1	3	6	4	7	2	5	9
5	4	2	1	8	9	6	3	7
6	9	7	2	3	5	8	1	4

Puzzle 241

5	1	2	3	4	8	7	6	9
6	9	4	1	5	7	3	2	8
8	3	7	6	2	9	1	5	4
1	8	6	9	7	4	2	3	5
4	5	9	2	3	1	6	8	7
2	7	3	8	6	5	9	4	1
3	4	8	7	9	6	5	1	2
9	6	5	4	1	2	8	7	3
7	2	1	5	8	3	4	9	6

Puzzle 242

6	9	5	7	4	2	8	3	1
7	3	4	8	9	1	2	6	5
1	2	8	6	3	5	4	7	9
2	8	7	5	1	9	6	4	3
9	5	3	4	2	6	1	8	7
4	6	1	3	7	8	9	5	2
5	1	6	2	8	7	3	9	4
3	7	9	1	6	4	5	2	8
8	4	2	9	5	3	7	1	6

Puzzle 243

8	7	6	5	3	4	1	9	2
3	2	4	1	7	9	6	8	5
1	9	5	6	2	8	4	7	3
4	8	9	7	6	2	3	5	1
2	3	1	4	8	5	7	6	9
6	5	7	3	9	1	2	4	8
9	1	8	2	4	7	5	3	6
5	4	3	8	1	6	9	2	7
7	6	2	9	5	3	8	1	4

Puzzle 244

9	2	8	3	4	5	7	6	1
1	3	7	2	6	8	9	5	4
4	6	5	9	1	7	3	2	8
8	4	3	1	2	6	5	9	7
5	1	2	8	7	9	6	4	3
6	7	9	4	5	3	1	8	2
7	9	4	5	8	1	2	3	6
3	8	6	7	9	2	4	1	5
2	5	1	6	3	4	8	7	9

Puzzle 245

3	4	5	9	7	2	1	8	6
7	6	8	5	3	1	4	2	9
9	1	2	8	6	4	5	7	3
1	8	4	7	5	3	6	9	2
2	7	9	6	1	8	3	4	5
5	3	6	4	2	9	7	1	8
6	2	1	3	8	7	9	5	4
4	5	7	2	9	6	8	3	1
8	9	3	1	4	5	2	6	7

Puzzle 246

8	3	2	1	4	9	7	5	6
7	9	1	2	6	5	8	4	3
5	4	6	3	8	7	1	9	2
3	7	4	5	1	6	9	2	8
2	6	9	7	3	8	5	1	4
1	8	5	4	9	2	6	3	7
9	5	7	6	2	3	4	8	1
6	1	3	8	5	4	2	7	9
4	2	8	9	7	1	3	6	5

Puzzle 247

6	7	2	3	9	1	8	5	4
1	9	3	8	4	5	2	7	6
5	4	8	6	7	2	9	3	1
8	5	4	7	6	3	1	9	2
7	1	6	2	5	9	3	4	8
2	3	9	4	1	8	7	6	5
4	8	1	9	3	6	5	2	7
3	2	7	5	8	4	6	1	9
9	6	5	1	2	7	4	8	3

Puzzle 248

8	4	5	3	6	9	7	1	2
9	3	1	5	2	7	8	4	6
2	7	6	4	1	8	5	9	3
7	5	2	9	4	1	3	6	8
3	9	8	7	5	6	1	2	4
6	1	4	2	8	3	9	7	5
5	2	3	1	7	4	6	8	9
1	6	9	8	3	2	4	5	7
4	8	7	6	9	5	2	3	1

249

6	8	9	4	7	5	1	2	3
4	3	1	8	9	2	7	5	6
5	2	7	3	1	6	4	9	8
1	4	3	7	8	9	2	6	5
2	6	8	5	4	1	9	3	7
7	9	5	2	6	3	8	1	4
3	7	2	9	5	4	6	8	1
8	5	6	1	2	7	3	4	9
9	1	4	6	3	8	5	7	2

250

7	1	2	9	8	5	3	4	6
8	4	3	2	7	6	5	9	1
5	9	6	1	4	3	2	8	7
4	8	7	6	9	2	1	3	5
6	3	1	7	5	4	9	2	8
9	2	5	3	1	8	7	6	4
3	6	8	5	2	7	4	1	9
2	5	9	4	6	1	8	7	3
1	7	4	8	3	9	6	5	2

251

4	2	1	8	5	7	3	9	6
6	5	3	4	2	9	7	8	1
8	9	7	1	6	3	2	4	5
5	4	8	9	7	2	6	1	3
7	1	9	6	3	8	5	2	4
3	6	2	5	1	4	8	7	9
1	8	5	2	4	6	9	3	7
2	7	6	3	9	1	4	5	8
9	3	4	7	8	5	1	6	2

252

1	9	7	3	4	2	6	5	8
5	2	3	8	9	6	4	7	1
4	6	8	7	5	1	2	3	9
2	4	1	9	6	5	7	8	3
6	7	5	4	8	3	1	9	2
3	8	9	1	2	7	5	6	4
8	3	2	5	7	4	9	1	6
9	5	4	6	1	8	3	2	7
7	1	6	2	3	9	8	4	5

253

7	3	8	2	9	6	1	4	5
2	1	9	5	3	4	7	6	8
4	5	6	8	1	7	3	9	2
3	7	4	9	2	8	6	5	1
5	8	2	4	6	1	9	3	7
6	9	1	7	5	3	8	2	4
8	2	7	3	4	9	5	1	6
9	6	5	1	8	2	4	7	3
1	4	3	6	7	5	2	8	9

254

8	6	4	5	2	7	1	9	3
2	7	1	4	9	3	8	6	5
3	5	9	6	8	1	4	7	2
7	2	3	8	5	4	9	1	6
5	9	6	1	7	2	3	8	4
1	4	8	9	3	6	2	5	7
4	3	5	7	1	8	6	2	9
9	8	2	3	6	5	7	4	1
6	1	7	2	4	9	5	3	8

255

8	4	1	3	6	9	7	5	2
2	6	3	1	7	5	8	4	9
7	5	9	8	4	2	1	3	6
1	2	7	4	9	6	5	8	3
9	3	6	7	5	8	4	2	1
5	8	4	2	1	3	6	9	7
6	1	2	9	8	4	3	7	5
3	7	8	5	2	1	9	6	4
4	9	5	6	3	7	2	1	8

256

1	3	5	8	9	2	7	4	6
9	6	7	5	4	3	8	2	1
4	8	2	1	7	6	9	5	3
2	4	6	7	1	5	3	9	8
5	1	3	9	2	8	4	6	7
8	7	9	6	3	4	5	1	2
6	5	4	3	8	1	2	7	9
3	9	1	2	5	7	6	8	4
7	2	8	4	6	9	1	3	5

257

1	5	2	9	7	4	6	3	8
7	3	8	2	1	6	9	4	5
4	6	9	8	5	3	2	7	1
2	7	3	1	6	9	5	8	4
9	8	5	3	4	2	7	1	6
6	4	1	7	8	5	3	9	2
8	9	4	6	2	7	1	5	3
3	1	6	5	9	8	4	2	7
5	2	7	4	3	1	8	6	9

258

1	9	5	7	3	4	8	6	2
7	8	4	1	6	2	9	3	5
6	2	3	5	9	8	1	4	7
9	1	6	3	2	7	5	8	4
8	4	2	6	5	1	3	7	9
3	5	7	8	4	9	6	2	1
2	6	1	4	8	5	7	9	3
4	7	8	9	1	3	2	5	6
5	3	9	2	7	6	4	1	8

259

6	1	3	9	5	2	8	7	4
4	5	7	3	6	8	1	9	2
9	8	2	4	1	7	5	6	3
8	2	4	6	7	9	3	5	1
3	7	1	5	8	4	6	2	9
5	9	6	1	2	3	4	8	7
2	4	8	7	3	6	9	1	5
1	6	9	2	4	5	7	3	8
7	3	5	8	9	1	2	4	6

260

9	5	2	7	4	6	1	8	3
7	6	1	9	3	8	5	4	2
3	8	4	5	2	1	9	7	6
8	1	6	3	9	4	2	5	7
5	3	9	8	7	2	6	1	4
4	2	7	6	1	5	3	9	8
2	4	8	1	6	9	7	3	5
1	7	5	2	8	3	4	6	9
6	9	3	4	5	7	8	2	1

261

1	5	8	7	3	2	4	6	9
3	9	7	6	4	1	5	2	8
6	2	4	5	9	8	1	7	3
2	7	9	8	5	6	3	4	1
5	8	6	4	1	3	7	9	2
4	1	3	9	2	7	8	5	6
7	4	2	1	8	9	6	3	5
8	3	5	2	6	4	9	1	7
9	6	1	3	7	5	2	8	4

262

8	4	5	1	3	7	6	2	9
1	3	9	2	4	6	8	7	5
7	6	2	9	8	5	1	4	3
2	7	4	3	6	1	5	9	8
9	5	3	4	2	8	7	6	1
6	8	1	5	7	9	2	3	4
4	2	6	8	1	3	9	5	7
3	9	8	7	5	2	4	1	6
5	1	7	6	9	4	3	8	2

263

1	4	2	8	5	7	9	3	6
5	9	3	2	4	6	8	7	1
6	7	8	9	3	1	4	2	5
2	3	4	1	9	8	5	6	7
8	1	5	6	7	4	3	9	2
9	6	7	3	2	5	1	4	8
7	2	9	5	8	3	6	1	4
4	5	1	7	6	9	2	8	3
3	8	6	4	1	2	7	5	9

264

1	3	5	8	7	9	4	6	2
6	8	2	1	5	4	9	7	3
9	7	4	3	6	2	8	5	1
8	9	1	2	3	7	5	4	6
3	4	6	9	1	5	2	8	7
5	2	7	4	8	6	1	3	9
2	5	3	6	9	8	7	1	4
4	6	8	7	2	1	3	9	5
7	1	9	5	4	3	6	2	8

Grid 265

6	2	5	9	1	3	4	8	7
9	8	4	7	5	6	2	3	1
7	1	3	4	8	2	9	5	6
4	3	9	6	2	1	5	7	8
2	7	8	5	3	4	1	6	9
1	5	6	8	9	7	3	4	2
8	6	1	2	4	5	7	9	3
3	4	7	1	6	9	8	2	5
5	9	2	3	7	8	6	1	4

Grid 266

2	3	8	1	4	7	9	5	6
5	1	6	2	8	9	4	3	7
7	4	9	6	5	3	2	8	1
3	8	5	4	1	6	7	2	9
4	7	2	5	9	8	1	6	3
9	6	1	7	3	2	5	4	8
8	5	4	9	6	1	3	7	2
1	2	3	8	7	4	6	9	5
6	9	7	3	2	5	8	1	4

Grid 267

9	7	4	8	3	2	5	6	1
2	5	3	9	1	6	7	8	4
8	1	6	7	4	5	2	3	9
6	4	9	2	5	7	3	1	8
3	8	7	1	6	9	4	2	5
5	2	1	4	8	3	9	7	6
1	9	8	3	2	4	6	5	7
7	6	2	5	9	1	8	4	3
4	3	5	6	7	8	1	9	2

Grid 268

6	5	1	3	2	9	7	4	8
8	9	4	6	5	7	3	2	1
2	3	7	4	1	8	6	5	9
4	8	9	5	3	2	1	7	6
7	6	3	1	8	4	2	9	5
5	1	2	7	9	6	4	8	3
9	7	6	8	4	3	5	1	2
3	2	5	9	7	1	8	6	4
1	4	8	2	6	5	9	3	7

Grid 269

6	9	5	7	3	1	8	2	4
2	4	3	6	8	9	7	1	5
7	1	8	2	5	4	6	3	9
3	5	1	8	9	6	4	7	2
9	6	2	1	4	7	3	5	8
4	8	7	5	2	3	9	6	1
8	3	6	9	1	5	2	4	7
5	2	4	3	7	8	1	9	6
1	7	9	4	6	2	5	8	3

Grid 270

7	2	6	9	3	5	4	8	1
1	9	4	2	8	7	3	5	6
5	3	8	6	1	4	2	7	9
3	1	2	5	9	8	6	4	7
9	8	5	4	7	6	1	2	3
6	4	7	3	2	1	5	9	8
2	5	9	8	6	3	7	1	4
8	6	1	7	4	2	9	3	5
4	7	3	1	5	9	8	6	2

Grid 271

7	9	6	4	2	3	1	5	8
8	3	1	7	5	9	2	4	6
5	4	2	1	6	8	9	3	7
6	1	5	9	7	2	3	8	4
4	2	9	3	8	5	7	6	1
3	7	8	6	4	1	5	2	9
2	5	7	8	9	6	4	1	3
9	6	3	5	1	4	8	7	2
1	8	4	2	3	7	6	9	5

Grid 272

8	6	9	3	1	7	5	2	4
1	7	3	2	4	5	6	9	8
2	5	4	6	9	8	1	3	7
5	8	7	1	3	6	9	4	2
6	9	2	7	8	4	3	5	1
4	3	1	5	2	9	8	7	6
9	1	8	4	5	2	7	6	3
3	4	6	9	7	1	2	8	5
7	2	5	8	6	3	4	1	9

273

9	1	8	2	3	4	7	5	6
5	6	2	7	9	1	4	3	8
7	3	4	5	6	8	1	2	9
6	4	9	8	7	5	3	1	2
2	7	5	9	1	3	8	6	4
1	8	3	6	4	2	5	9	7
4	9	6	3	5	7	2	8	1
3	2	7	1	8	9	6	4	5
8	5	1	4	2	6	9	7	3

274

9	7	2	6	1	8	3	5	4
1	6	5	2	4	3	9	7	8
3	8	4	7	5	9	6	1	2
4	5	6	9	7	2	1	8	3
7	9	8	5	3	1	2	4	6
2	3	1	4	8	6	5	9	7
6	1	3	8	9	7	4	2	5
5	2	7	1	6	4	8	3	9
8	4	9	3	2	5	7	6	1

275

9	2	1	6	5	3	8	7	4
7	8	4	9	1	2	6	5	3
3	5	6	7	4	8	2	9	1
2	9	8	3	7	5	4	1	6
4	3	7	8	6	1	5	2	9
6	1	5	2	9	4	3	8	7
8	4	2	1	3	9	7	6	5
1	6	3	5	2	7	9	4	8
5	7	9	4	8	6	1	3	2

276

2	4	5	8	1	7	9	3	6
8	1	9	4	6	3	5	2	7
7	3	6	5	2	9	8	1	4
9	2	4	3	7	8	1	6	5
5	7	8	6	9	1	3	4	2
3	6	1	2	4	5	7	8	9
1	8	2	7	5	6	4	9	3
6	5	3	9	8	4	2	7	1
4	9	7	1	3	2	6	5	8

277

2	7	4	6	8	1	5	3	9
6	5	3	7	4	9	1	2	8
9	8	1	3	5	2	7	4	6
7	2	5	4	3	8	6	9	1
3	1	9	2	6	5	4	8	7
4	6	8	1	9	7	3	5	2
8	9	6	5	7	4	2	1	3
1	4	7	9	2	3	8	6	5
5	3	2	8	1	6	9	7	4

278

3	7	5	4	9	2	6	8	1
4	2	9	6	1	8	5	7	3
8	1	6	7	3	5	9	2	4
2	8	7	1	5	6	4	3	9
6	9	4	8	7	3	2	1	5
1	5	3	2	4	9	8	6	7
5	4	8	3	2	1	7	9	6
9	3	2	5	6	7	1	4	8
7	6	1	9	8	4	3	5	2

279

5	2	4	3	8	9	7	6	1
1	7	6	5	4	2	3	8	9
9	8	3	7	6	1	5	4	2
7	9	5	1	2	8	6	3	4
4	3	1	9	7	6	8	2	5
8	6	2	4	3	5	9	1	7
3	4	8	2	9	7	1	5	6
6	5	9	8	1	4	2	7	3
2	1	7	6	5	3	4	9	8

280

3	9	1	4	8	6	7	2	5
4	2	6	1	5	7	3	8	9
5	8	7	9	3	2	4	1	6
9	4	5	7	2	1	6	3	8
2	7	8	3	6	4	9	5	1
6	1	3	5	9	8	2	7	4
8	3	4	6	7	5	1	9	2
7	6	2	8	1	9	5	4	3
1	5	9	2	4	3	8	6	7

281

5	3	9	6	8	2	4	7	1
4	8	1	9	7	3	2	6	5
6	2	7	1	4	5	8	3	9
9	4	6	2	1	7	5	8	3
7	1	8	5	3	4	6	9	2
2	5	3	8	9	6	1	4	7
8	9	4	7	5	1	3	2	6
3	6	5	4	2	9	7	1	8
1	7	2	3	6	8	9	5	4

282

4	1	6	8	3	7	2	9	5
7	3	9	6	2	5	1	4	8
5	2	8	9	4	1	6	3	7
3	5	4	2	6	8	9	7	1
1	8	7	3	5	9	4	2	6
9	6	2	1	7	4	5	8	3
8	9	3	4	1	6	7	5	2
2	7	1	5	9	3	8	6	4
6	4	5	7	8	2	3	1	9

283

9	4	3	5	1	2	6	7	8
8	6	1	9	4	7	5	2	3
5	7	2	3	8	6	4	9	1
1	5	7	6	2	3	9	8	4
3	9	4	8	7	5	1	6	2
6	2	8	1	9	4	3	5	7
2	1	5	4	6	8	7	3	9
4	8	6	7	3	9	2	1	5
7	3	9	2	5	1	8	4	6

284

8	2	4	9	1	5	3	6	7
6	1	5	8	3	7	9	4	2
3	7	9	6	4	2	1	5	8
9	6	1	2	5	8	4	7	3
4	5	8	3	7	9	2	1	6
7	3	2	1	6	4	8	9	5
1	8	7	5	9	3	6	2	4
2	4	6	7	8	1	5	3	9
5	9	3	4	2	6	7	8	1

285

8	7	4	2	3	6	1	9	5
1	5	6	9	4	7	2	3	8
3	2	9	1	8	5	6	4	7
4	6	3	8	5	2	9	7	1
9	1	2	6	7	4	8	5	3
7	8	5	3	1	9	4	6	2
6	4	7	5	2	1	3	8	9
2	9	8	7	6	3	5	1	4
5	3	1	4	9	8	7	2	6

286

9	4	3	6	7	2	8	1	5
6	1	8	9	4	5	7	3	2
5	7	2	8	3	1	6	9	4
8	6	9	4	5	3	1	2	7
7	3	5	1	2	6	4	8	9
1	2	4	7	9	8	3	5	6
4	9	1	2	8	7	5	6	3
2	5	6	3	1	4	9	7	8
3	8	7	5	6	9	2	4	1

287

7	2	8	1	4	9	6	3	5
9	4	6	5	2	3	7	8	1
5	1	3	7	8	6	9	4	2
4	3	2	6	1	5	8	7	9
8	6	9	4	7	2	5	1	3
1	7	5	9	3	8	4	2	6
6	8	1	2	9	7	3	5	4
2	9	7	3	5	4	1	6	8
3	5	4	8	6	1	2	9	7

288

8	1	3	9	5	6	4	7	2
4	9	7	2	3	1	6	5	8
2	5	6	8	7	4	1	9	3
7	8	1	4	9	2	5	3	6
5	2	9	3	6	7	8	4	1
3	6	4	1	8	5	7	2	9
6	4	8	5	2	3	9	1	7
9	3	5	7	1	8	2	6	4
1	7	2	6	4	9	3	8	5

289

1	8	3	6	9	5	4	7	2
6	4	7	2	1	3	5	9	8
9	5	2	8	4	7	3	6	1
4	6	8	9	5	2	7	1	3
2	7	5	4	3	1	9	8	6
3	1	9	7	6	8	2	5	4
8	9	6	3	7	4	1	2	5
5	2	4	1	8	9	6	3	7
7	3	1	5	2	6	8	4	9

290

7	8	1	5	2	9	4	3	6
6	9	2	1	3	4	7	5	8
3	4	5	7	6	8	1	9	2
1	7	6	4	5	3	2	8	9
9	5	4	2	8	1	6	7	3
2	3	8	9	7	6	5	4	1
5	6	3	8	1	7	9	2	4
4	1	7	3	9	2	8	6	5
8	2	9	6	4	5	3	1	7

291

9	5	7	4	8	2	3	1	6
8	2	6	9	3	1	4	5	7
1	3	4	6	7	5	9	8	2
2	7	3	5	6	4	8	9	1
4	9	8	7	1	3	6	2	5
6	1	5	8	2	9	7	4	3
7	8	9	2	5	6	1	3	4
3	4	2	1	9	7	5	6	8
5	6	1	3	4	8	2	7	9

292

8	1	9	5	7	4	6	2	3
5	3	2	8	1	6	7	4	9
7	4	6	3	2	9	5	1	8
1	2	4	7	9	8	3	5	6
3	6	8	4	5	2	1	9	7
9	7	5	1	6	3	2	8	4
6	8	7	2	4	5	9	3	1
4	5	1	9	3	7	8	6	2
2	9	3	6	8	1	4	7	5

293

9	5	3	4	7	1	2	8	6
1	6	8	2	3	5	9	7	4
7	4	2	6	9	8	1	3	5
6	3	7	8	2	4	5	9	1
8	9	4	1	5	3	7	6	2
5	2	1	7	6	9	8	4	3
4	7	6	9	1	2	3	5	8
2	8	5	3	4	7	6	1	9
3	1	9	5	8	6	4	2	7

294

1	4	9	8	5	2	3	7	6
8	6	2	1	3	7	5	4	9
3	7	5	9	6	4	8	1	2
6	8	4	2	7	3	1	9	5
5	9	7	6	4	1	2	8	3
2	1	3	5	9	8	7	6	4
9	5	1	7	2	6	4	3	8
7	3	6	4	8	5	9	2	1
4	2	8	3	1	9	6	5	7

295

4	6	9	5	2	8	7	1	3
7	8	3	1	6	9	2	5	4
5	1	2	3	7	4	9	8	6
8	5	1	7	4	6	3	2	9
2	7	4	8	9	3	5	6	1
3	9	6	2	5	1	4	7	8
1	4	7	6	3	5	8	9	2
9	2	8	4	1	7	6	3	5
6	3	5	9	8	2	1	4	7

296

5	9	2	4	6	3	7	1	8
8	1	4	9	7	2	6	3	5
7	3	6	8	1	5	4	9	2
4	7	9	2	3	1	5	8	6
2	6	8	7	5	9	3	4	1
3	5	1	6	8	4	2	7	9
9	8	5	3	2	7	1	6	4
6	2	7	1	4	8	9	5	3
1	4	3	5	9	6	8	2	7

297

6	5	3	1	9	7	4	2	8
4	7	9	3	2	8	1	5	6
2	8	1	5	4	6	7	3	9
5	2	7	9	8	1	3	6	4
3	1	4	6	7	5	9	8	2
9	6	8	2	3	4	5	1	7
7	3	6	8	5	9	2	4	1
8	9	5	4	1	2	6	7	3
1	4	2	7	6	3	8	9	5

298

3	7	4	8	1	9	2	5	6
5	6	9	4	7	2	3	8	1
8	2	1	5	6	3	9	4	7
1	4	7	2	8	5	6	3	9
9	3	5	1	4	6	8	7	2
6	8	2	9	3	7	4	1	5
4	1	6	7	9	8	5	2	3
2	9	8	3	5	1	7	6	4
7	5	3	6	2	4	1	9	8

299

9	6	7	3	5	2	1	8	4
4	2	8	9	6	1	7	5	3
1	3	5	4	8	7	9	2	6
5	7	1	8	9	4	3	6	2
2	9	4	7	3	6	5	1	8
3	8	6	1	2	5	4	7	9
8	4	2	5	1	9	6	3	7
6	5	9	2	7	3	8	4	1
7	1	3	6	4	8	2	9	5

300

5	6	7	8	3	9	4	2	1
4	9	3	7	1	2	8	6	5
2	1	8	4	6	5	3	7	9
8	5	4	3	9	7	6	1	2
3	2	6	1	5	4	9	8	7
9	7	1	6	2	8	5	4	3
1	4	5	2	8	3	7	9	6
6	8	9	5	7	1	2	3	4
7	3	2	9	4	6	1	5	8